BRIGHT & BOLD
Wool Appliqué

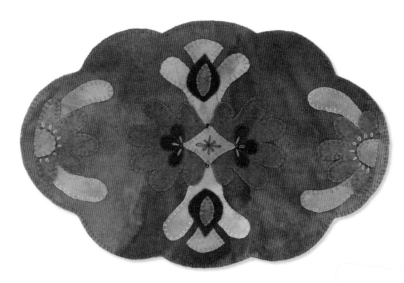

by
Angela Lawrence

D1709962

BRIGHT & BOLD
Wool Appliqué
by Angela Lawrence

This book was designed, produced,
and published by Landauer Publishing, LLC
3100 101st Street, Urbandale, IA 50322
515/287/2144   800/557/2144   landauerpub.com

President/Publisher: Jeramy Lanigan Landauer
Editor: Jeri Simon
Art Director: Laurel Albright
Photographer: Sue Voegtlin

Library of Congress: 2015952282

ISBN 13: 978-1-935726-81-4
This book printed on acid-free paper.
Printed in United States

10-9-8-7-6-5-4-3-2-1

PHOTOGRAPHY PERMISSION:
Polk County Master Gardeners/Altoona, IA
    Iowa State Extension Service
RS Welding Studio/Victor, IA
West End Salvage/Des Moines, IA
The Woolen Needle/Williamsburg, IA

 FACEBOOK.COM/LANDAUERPUBLISHING  YOUTUBE.COM/LANDAUERPUBLISHING PINTEREST.COM/LANDAUERPUB

Contents

Introduction

Wool Appliqué Basics

Projects

About the Author/ Acknowledgments/ Resources

Destination Wool

Enjoy the Journey

Introduction

Welcome to the expanding world of wool appliqué. With the growing surge in popularity, hand-dyed wool presents quilters with an opportunity to create intricate appliqué designs without worrying about raw edges fraying. Its soft texture provides exciting, new, creative opportunities in quilt design. Now available in a beautiful array of rich, vibrant colors, hand-dyed wools are screaming to be used in our quilt designs.

Today, the focus of design is pattern. We see repetitive designs in floor and wall coverings, as well as in drapery and upholstery. Each project illustrated in this book features intricate shapes, built upon each other and layered to create interesting, dynamic, textural patterns. From the simple to the more elaborate, these innovative wool projects will introduce you to a chic, new sophistication in the world of quilt design.

Quilting techniques are just as personal and unique as the created project. Wool techniques are no exception. In this book, I have included techniques that I am confident will help you successfully complete each of the projects. Experiment, have fun, and decide which techniques work best for you. There are also dozens of templates that can be used over and over again to create a vast array of projects.

I had a wonderful time creating these wool designs. May you enjoy your wool journey, have fun with each project, and remember it is all for the love of wool!

Angela

Understanding Wool

Wool is a natural fiber that comes from the fleece of sheep. After a sheep is sheared, the fleece fibers are washed to produce wool roving or raw wool. This roving is spun to produce thread, which is woven to create wool fabric.

Wool Felt vs. Felted Wool

The most commonly asked question among quilters is, "what is the difference between wool felt and felted wool?"

Wool felt is produced by matting and tightly condensing wool and synthetic fibers together. The fibers are subjected to moisture and heat before being compressed.

Felted wool is 100 percent woven wool that has gone through a process that shrinks and tightens the wool fibers. This creates a soft, supple wool fabric that is more resistant to fraying. In the felting process, the wool is first soaked in hot water and then immersed in very cold water. Next, it is placed in the dryer on a high heat setting. This process shocks and shrinks the wool fibers, which makes the edges of the wool less likely to fray.

Hand-dyed wool is felted wool. It has risen in popularity due to the wonderful varieties of colors that are available. When wool is dyed, it is put through a process similar to that of felted wool. To ensure it is felted, wool can be steam-ironed.

Wool purchased off the bolt has **not** gone through the felting process. For example, a yard of wool cut from the bolt will measure 36" x 54". After going through the felting process, wool will typically shrink 4" in all directions and end up measuring approximately 32" x 50". If you are unsure if a wool piece is felted, simply put it through the felting process.

Testing for Colorfastness

If you are concerned about the colorfastness of hand-dyed wool, test it by placing a small scrap of the wool in warm water with a swatch of white cotton fabric. If the wool is not colorfast, it will bleed onto the white cotton fabric. Steam ironing a piece of wool layered on white cotton fabric will also test for colorfastness.

Caring for Wool Quilts

Treat a wool quilt as you would any other quilt. For best results, wash the quilt by hand or on your washing machine's delicate cycle in cool water, using mild detergent or a gentle quilt soap. Include a color catching laundry sheet to protect against color bleeding and to help preserve the fabric's original colors. Lay the quilt flat to dry.

Wool provides variety in texture and dimension, especially when used with other fabrics. The projects in this book can be completed using wool appliqué pieces on a wool background, as well as using cotton, silk or linen as the background fabric. For larger projects, such as a lap-size or bed quilt, use a cotton background fabric with the wool appliqué to make the quilt lighter and less bulky.

Threads

A large selection of thread is available for wool appliqué. Knowing which thread to use can sometimes be confusing. While there really are no rules, I have included some guidelines concerning the variety of threads. Have fun experimenting with different threads.

Cotton Threads

Stranded Cotton

The most commonly used cotton thread is embroidery floss. It consists of a skein of six threads that can be separated according to your stitching needs. I generally use DMC Embroidery Floss, which is a colorfast Egyptian cotton that comes in a large variety of colors. To separate the strands, simply pull them apart one strand at a time. If using more than one strand, rejoin them to create a unified length.

When working with stranded cotton, the more strands you use, the heavier the final stitch. This needs to be considered before beginning to stitch. When stitching wool appliqué shapes to the background fabric, I use one strand for the whip stitch and two strands for the blanket stitch. Stranded cotton thread can also be used for embellishment stitches. Use one strand of floss for a very fine embroidery stitch. There are times when three strands of floss are necessary to create a heavy, raised decorative stitch.

Perle Cotton

Perle cotton is a nondivisible mercerized cotton thread. It is the twist of the threads that gives it the perle name. The thread comes in a range of sizes with the smallest number (3) being the thickest and the largest number (16) being the finest. Size 8 and 12 threads are most commonly used for stitching around the wool appliqué shapes.

Wool Threads

Wool threads have a slightly looser weave that blends beautifully into the edge of the wool appliqué shapes. It is a great thread to use for the whip stitch because the stitch disappears into the edge of the wool. Wool threads can also be used for embellishment stitches.

Notions and Supplies

A Chenille No. 24 is the perfect needle when working with wool. It has a large eye opening for threading and a sharp point that easily goes through the wool. An embroidery needle #10 will also be necessary when adding embellishment stitches to wool projects.

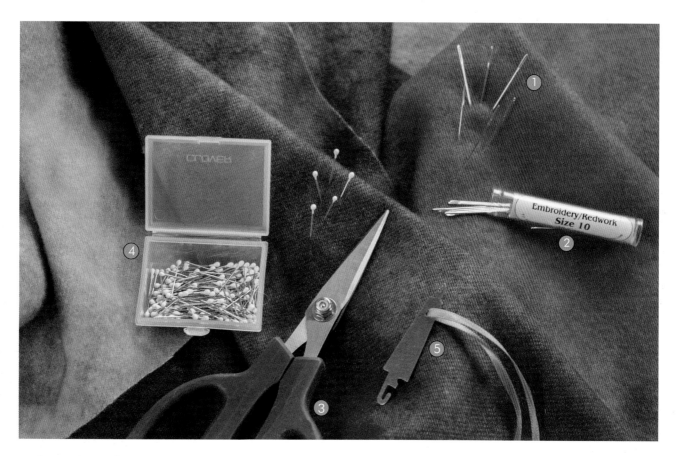

A few of my favorite basic tools—

1 Clover Gold Eye Chenille Needles (#24)—
Stitching wool appliqué shapes to background fabric

2 Embroidery Needles #10—
Adding decorative stitches to wool appliqué shapes

3 Famoré 6" Razor Edge Scissors with Large Ring Comfort Handle—
Cutting wool shapes precisely

4 Clover Appliqué Pins
(¾" white head appliqué pins)—
Securing wool appliqué shapes to the background fabric

5 Needle Threader by Lo Rain®—
Easily threads long-eye needles

Appliqué Preparation

Freezer Paper for Templates

When beginning a wool project, you must first create templates to transfer the appliqué shapes from the pattern to the felted wool. Freezer paper is a great product to use for templates because it is transparent enough to see through when tracing.

Follow the steps below when using freezer paper:

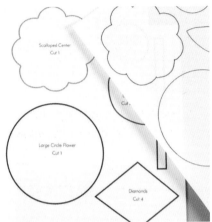  

1 Using a permanent marker, trace shapes onto the paper-side of the freezer paper. Leave space between each shape.

2 Using a paper scissors, cut out freezer paper shapes approximately 1/8" from the traced line.

3 Using a hot, dry iron, press shapes to the wool with the paper side up and the waxy side down.

Note: If there is a shape within the template marked "cut out", it is extra and can be discarded or saved for another project.

 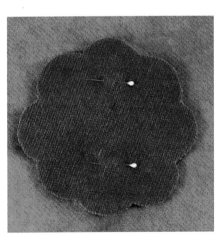 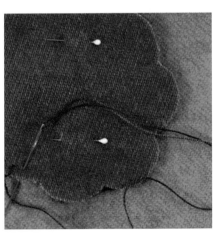

4 Cut out wool shapes along the traced line.

5 Remove the freezer paper and position the wool shape on the background fabric. Pin in place.

6 Stitch shapes to the background fabric.

Fusible Stabilizer

Using a paper-backed fusible stabilizer with wool is a good option, but not a necessity. The benefits, however, are worth the additional preparation steps. The need for freezer paper is eliminated when using paper-backed fusible products.

Fusible stabilizers are used to adhere the appliqué shapes to the background fabric by ironing, eliminating the need for pins. Lite Steam-A-Seam 2® and Soft Fuse Premium™ are two of my favorite fusible products because both will adhere wool shapes to a wool or cotton background. Many other fusible products are not strong enough to adhere wool to wool. They will, however, adhere wool to cotton.

Fusible products also stabilize the edges of the wool shapes. Most fusible stabilizers work well for this job. The fusible gives the wool shape a clean, crisp edge. Without the stabilizer, wool with a loose weave will have a tendency to fray along the edges when attempting to hand-stitch.

If you decide to use a fusible stabilizer, take time to read the manufacturer's instructions for best results. Different products require different heat settings and handling instructions.

Steps to follow when using a paper-backed fusible stabilizer:

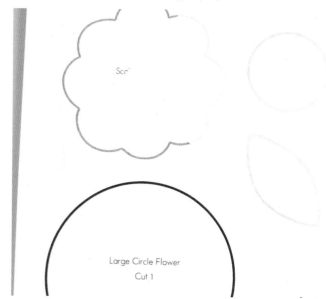

1 When using a fusible product reverse the appliqué design. Some appliqué patterns include the reversed design, so be sure to check before tracing.

2 Using a permanent marker, trace the design onto the paper-side of the fusible leaving space between each shape.

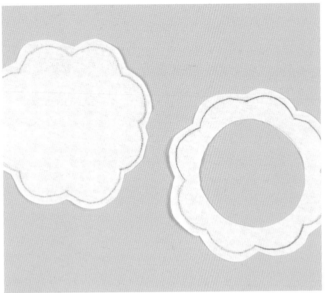

3 Using a paper scissors, cut out the shapes approximately 1/8" from the traced line. For larger appliqué shapes, or when pieces will be layered, window the template by cutting out the center of the shape. This step eliminates stiffness but still fuses the edges.

4 With the paper side up, iron fusible to the wool.

5 Cut out the wool shapes on the traced line. Note: Do not cut the windowed, or inner, portion of the shape.

6 Tear off the fusible paper, position the wool appliqué shape (fusible side down) on the wool or cotton background and iron in place. Stitch the shape to the background.
Note: Some stabilizers are not heavy enough to adhere to a wool background in which case appliqué pins will be needed.

Layered Shapes

When working with a detailed appliqué design, the appliqué shapes are often layered. This means that one shape rests on top of or is partially layered on another shape. The layering will determine the order in which shapes are sewn to the background. When layering occurs, it is necessary to add 1/4" seam allowance to the wool piece that will be tucked under another wool shape. All layered shapes in the projects in this book have a 1/4" seam allowance added. Follow the placement diagrams to layer the shapes.

Stitches

The blanket and whip stitch are two of the most commonly used stitches for attaching wool appliqué shapes to the background fabric.

Blanket Stitch

The blanket stitch gives a nice finished look to the wool edge. It is a decorative stitch with a raised appearance. Use a two-strand embroidery floss or a size 8 or 12 perle cotton thread. The color of your thread can match the color of the appliqué fabric or use a complementary color to enhance the appliqué. The size of the stitch should be proportional to the size of the wool appliqué shape. For example, the smaller the wool shape, the smaller the blanket stitch. Through experience you will learn to visually control the size and depth of the blanket stitch.

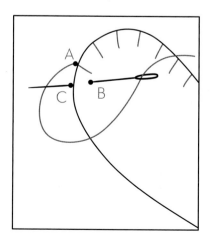

Whip Stitch

The whip stitch is used as a utility stitch and not as a decorative stitch. It is often used on small appliqué wool pieces that do not have room for a more decorative stitch. It works well in conjunction with other decorative stitches. Use one strand of embroidery floss or a size 12 perle cotton or wool thread. The thread color should match the color of the appliqué shape.

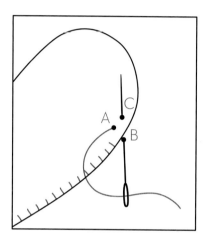

Inside/Outside Points

Whether using the blanket or whip stitch, stitch the inside and outside points in the following manner.

Place a stitch directly on the inside point.

Place a stitch directly on the outside point to ensure the point lies flat.

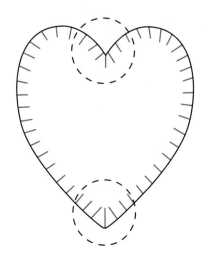

Embellishment

After the wool appliqué shapes have been stitched in place, it is time to add decorative stitches to further embellish the design. There are countless stitches available to embellish the wool appliqué.

Beads can also enhance and add a bit of fun to a wool design. Beads come in a variety of sizes. For smaller beads it will be necessary to use a finer needle such as a straw or bead needle.

Diagrams of Decorative Stitches

Chain Stitch

Feather Stitch

Fern Stitch

Closed Buttonhole Stitch

Running Stitch

Lazy Daisy Stitch

French Knot

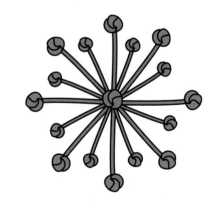

Pistil Stitch

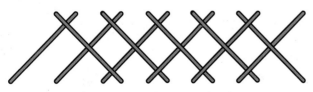

Herringbone Stitch

Stem Stitch

Woolen Tiles

A Set of Wool Coasters

Finished Size: 4-1/2" x 4-1/2"

This set of eight coasters takes on the appearance of painted porcelain tiles when placed together. A sturdy interlining makes them durable as well as functional. The colorful coasters are the perfect complement to any home décor.

Materials

Wool Requirements
Coaster Fronts: 12" x 20" rectangle

Coaster Backs: 12" x 20" rectangle

Wool Appliqué Requirements
Lime Green: 10" square

Burnt Orange: 10" square

Orange: 10" square

Raspberry: 10" square

Magenta: 10" square

Salmon: 10" square

Appliqué Patterns
Pages 16-19

Additional Materials
1 Craft Pack of Interlining by Craf-Tex

Floss, perle cotton or wool threads

Chenille needle size 24

Refer to pages 6-12 before beginning the project.

Cutting Instructions

From coaster front wool, cut:
  (8) 4-1/2" squares

From coaster back wool, cut:
  (8) 4-1/2" squares

From interlining, cut:
  (8) 4" squares

Preparing the Appliqué

1. Using the shapes on pages 16-19 and referring to pages 8-10, prepare the appliqué shapes. Use up to three colors to complete each appliqué design on the eight coasters.

2. Place sets of shapes on the 4-1/2" coaster fronts.

3. Stitch the shapes to the coaster fronts. Refer to pages 11-12 for stitching ideas.

Assembly Instructions

1. Layer the appliquéd wool coaster front, interlining and back.

2. Blanket stitch the edges to secure the three layers together.

Cut Lines ▬▬▬▬
Overlay Lines - - - - - - - - - -

Coaster 1

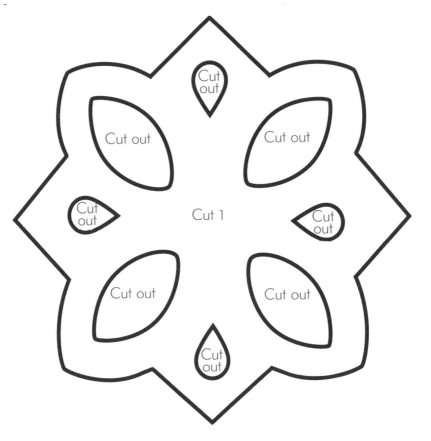

Cut out

Cut out

Cut out

Cut
out

Cut 1

Cut
out

Cut out

Cut out

Cut
out

Coaster 2

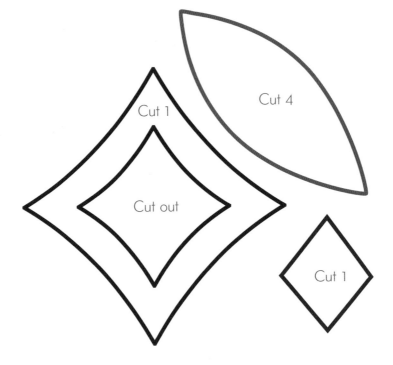

Cut 4

Cut 1

Cut out

Cut 1

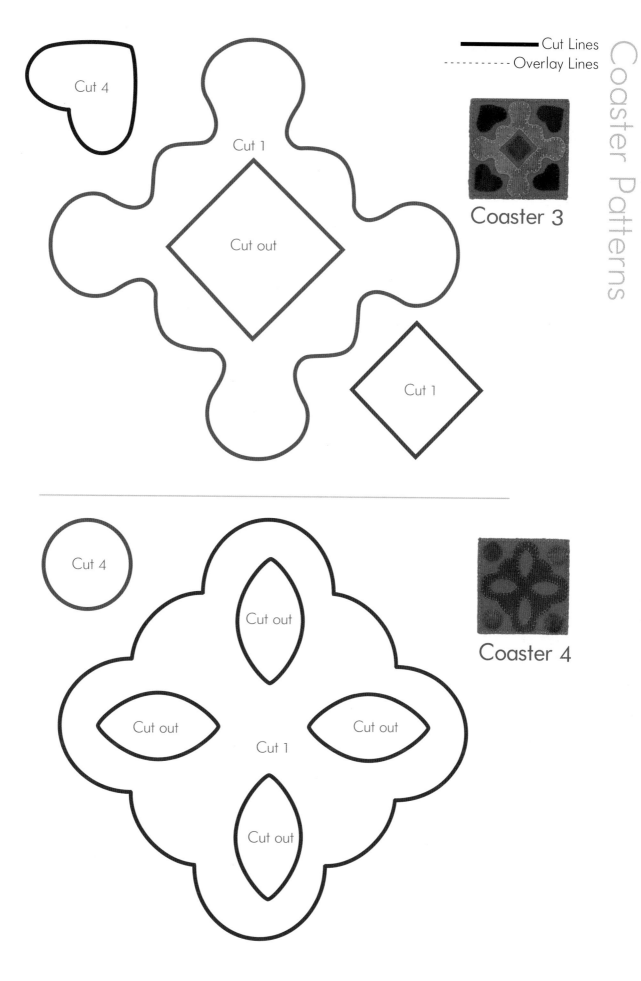

Cut Lines
Overlay Lines

Cut 4

Cut 1

Cut out

Cut 1

Coaster 3

Cut 4

Cut out

Cut out

Cut out

Cut 1

Cut out

Coaster 4

Cut Lines ━━━━━

Overlay Lines ----------

Coaster 5

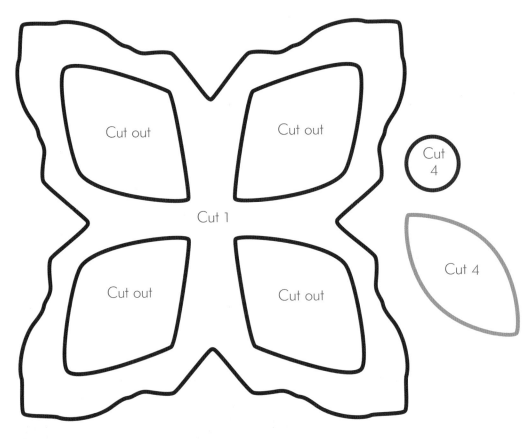

Cut out

Cut out

Cut 1

Cut out

Cut out

Cut 4

Cut 4

Coaster 6

Coaster 7

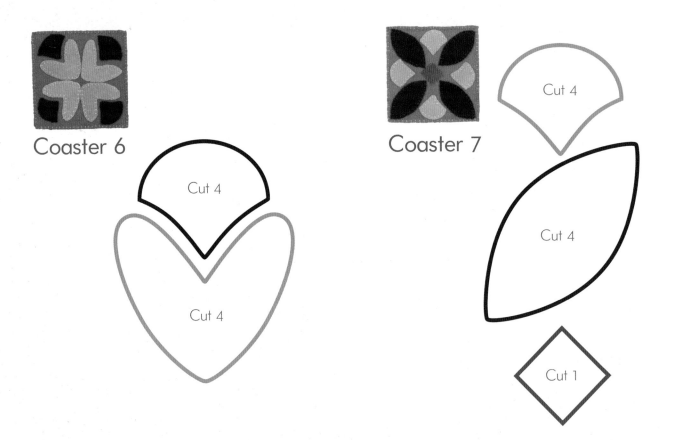

Cut 4

Cut 4

Cut 4

Cut 4

Cut 4

Cut 1

Cut Lines
- - - - - - - - Overlay Lines

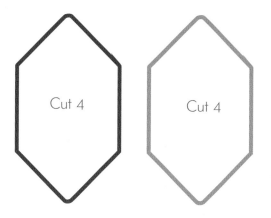

Cut 4

Cut 4

Coaster 8

Chevron Garden

A Wool Banner

Finished Size: 12" x 12"

This darling banner is small in size but will add a big splash of color to any space. The geometric shapes create a welcoming, happy chevron garden. Embellish the banner with buttons and beads.

Materials

Choose your own project colors or refer to the photo on page 20 for ideas.

Wool
Banner Front: 13" x 16" rectangle
Banner Back: 13" x 16" rectangle

Wool Appliqué
Large Circle Flower: 4" square
Scalloped Center: 4" square
Large Circle Center: 3" square
Small Circle Flowers: 7" square
Star Centers: 6" square
Small Circle Centers: 3" square
Stems: 3" x 6" rectangle
Leaves: 6" square
Chevron: 4" x 13" rectangle
Diamonds: 8" square

Appliqué Patterns
Pages 22-23

Additional Materials
3 small buttons
Assorted beads
Floss, perle cotton or wool threads
Chenille needle size 24
Straw needle for bead embellishing

Refer to pages 6-12 before beginning the project.

Cutting Instructions

From banner front wool, cut:
 (1) 12" square

From banner back wool, cut:
 (1) 12" square

Preparing the Appliqué

1. Using the shapes on pages 22-23 and referring to pages 8-10, prepare the appliqué shapes.

2. Referring to the photo on page 20, place the shapes on the 12" banner front.

3. Stitch the shapes to the banner front. Refer to pages 11-12 for stitching ideas.

4. Embellish the appliqué shapes with buttons and beads.

Assembly Instructions

1. Layer the appliquéd banner front and banner back together.

2. Trim the bottom edge of the banner 3/8" from the appliqué diamonds.

3. Blanket stitch around the edges of the banner to secure the layers in place.

Chevron Garden Patterns

Cut Lines
Overlay Lines

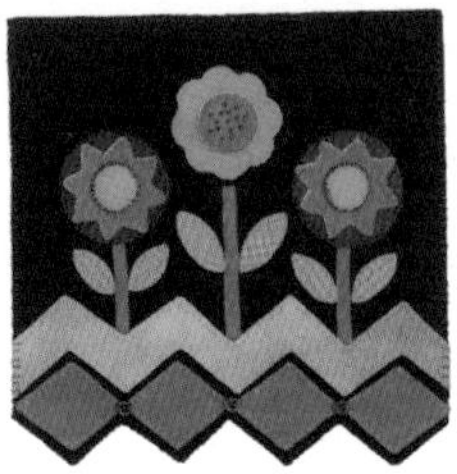

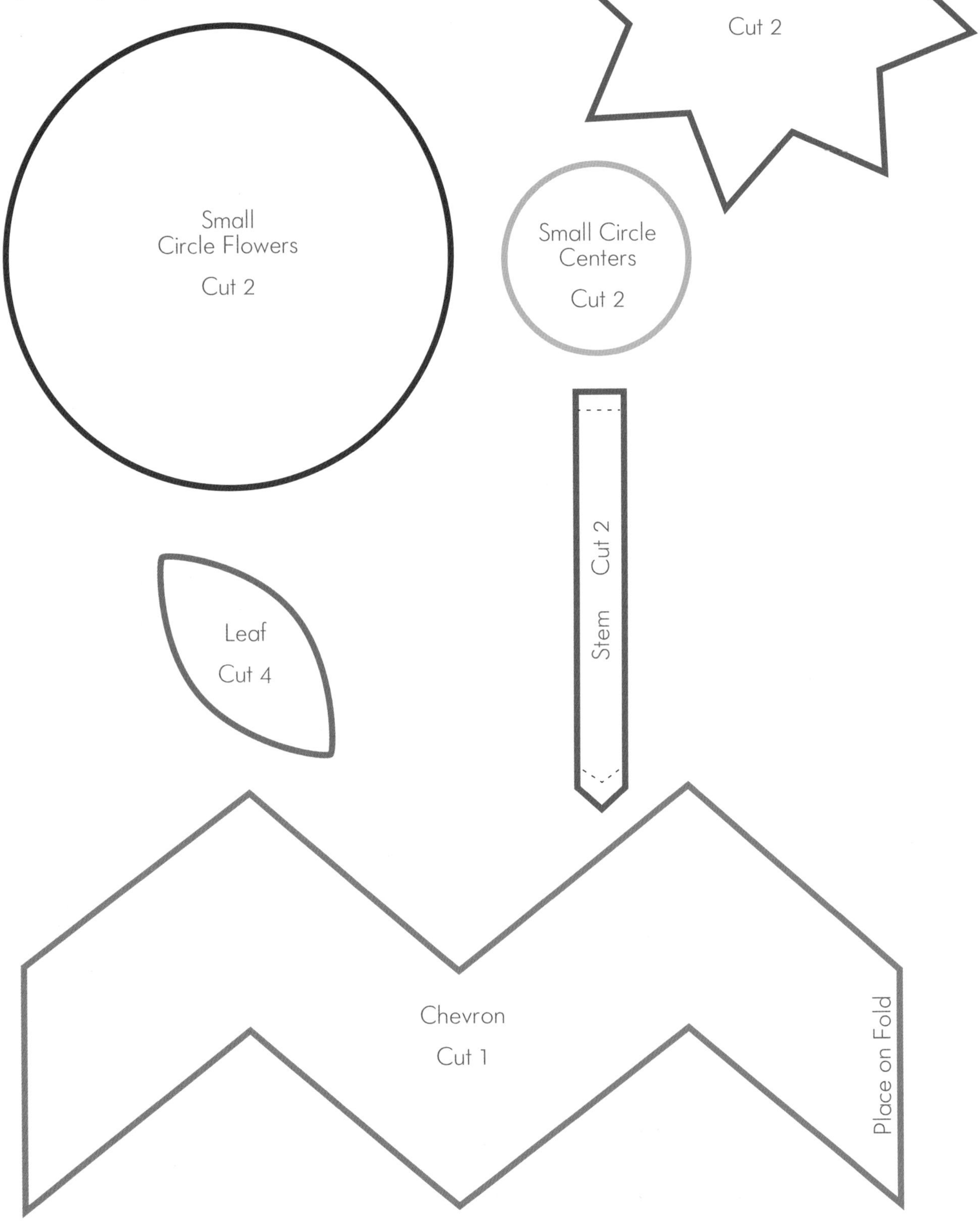
Star Centers
Cut 2
Small
Circle Flowers
Cut 2
Small Circle
Centers
Cut 2
Stem Cut 2
Leaf
Cut 4
Chevron
Cut 1
Place on Fold

Cut Lines
- - - - - - - Overlay Lines

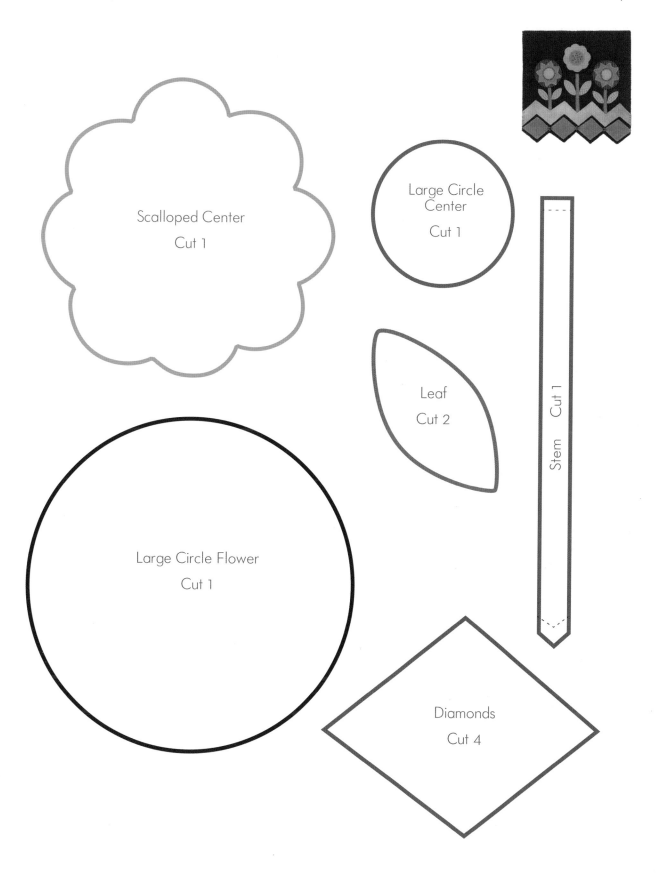

Scalloped Center
Cut 1

Large Circle
Center
Cut 1

Leaf
Cut 2

Stem   Cut 1

Large Circle Flower
Cut 1

Diamonds
Cut 4

Jeweled Sunrise

A Wool Candle Mat

Finished Size: 9" x 20"

This decorative candle mat will add a splash of color to any table. The mirrored symmetrical design consists of a lovely collage of shapes that create a beautiful unified design.

Materials

Wool

Candle Mat Front: 10" x 22" rectangle

Candle Mat Back: 10" x 22" rectangle

Wool Appliqué

Turquoise: 6" square

Red: 6" square

Aqua: 6" square

Green: 6" square

Mint: 6" square

Pink: 6" square

Appliqué Patterns

Pages 26 and 28-29

Additional Materials

Freezer paper

Floss, perle cotton or wool threads

Chenille needle size 24

Fusible stabilizer (optional)

Refer to pages 6-12 before beginning the project.

Preparing the Appliqué

1. Using freezer paper and the template on page 26, cut out the candle mat front and back. Refer to page 8 for information on using freezer paper.

2. Using the shapes on pages 28-29 and referring to pages 8-10, prepare the appliqué shapes.

3. Place the shapes on the candle mat front referring to page 27 for placement.

4. Stitch the appliqué shapes to the candle mat front. Refer to pages 11-12 for stitching ideas.

Assembly Instructions

1. Layer and pin the candle mat front and back together.

2. Blanket stitch around the edges of the candle mat to secure the layers in place.

Cut Lines ━━━━━━
Overlay Lines - - - - - - - - -

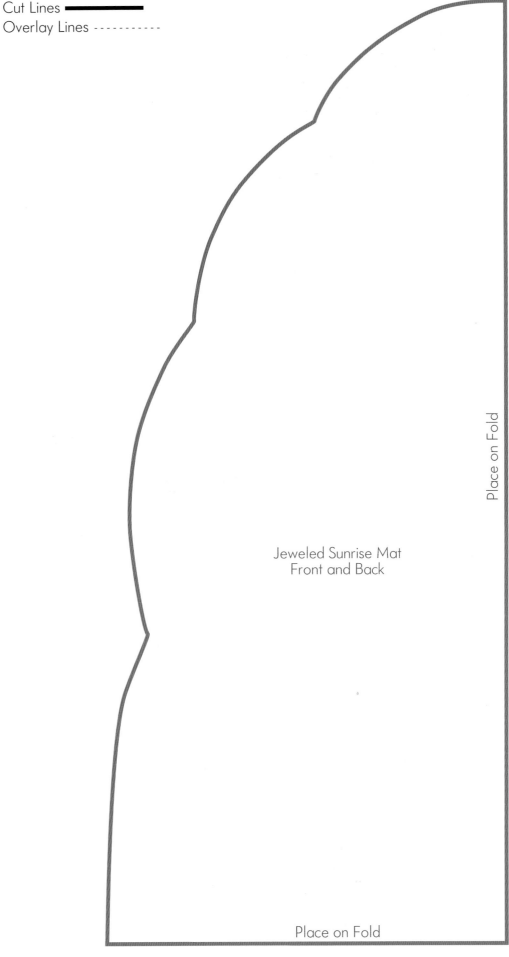

Jeweled Sunrise Mat
Front and Back

Place on Fold

Place on Fold

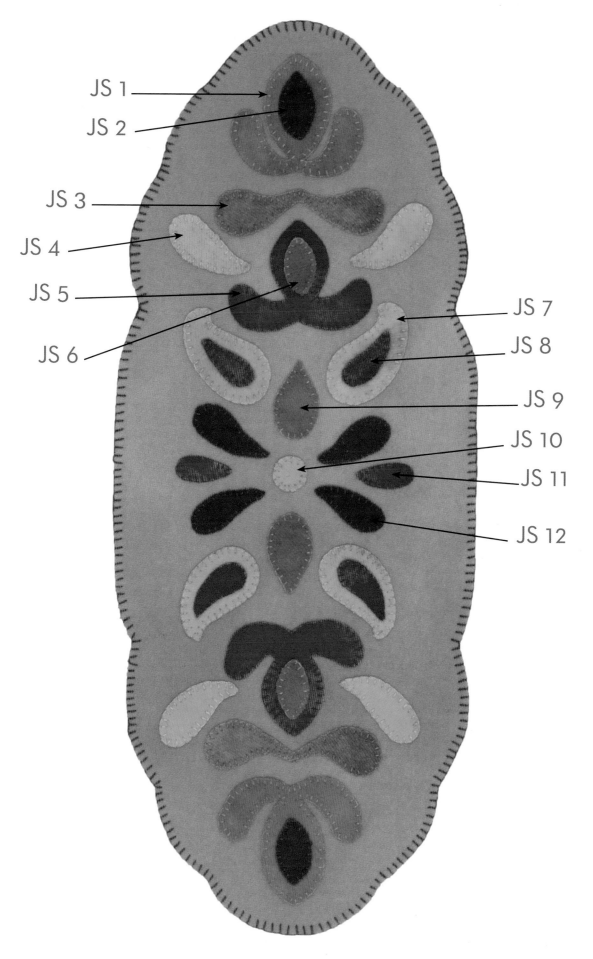

JS 1

JS 2

JS 3

JS 4

JS 5

JS 6

JS 7

JS 8

JS 9

JS 10

JS 11

JS 12

Jeweled Sunrise Patterns

Cut Lines ▬▬▬
Overlay Lines ----------

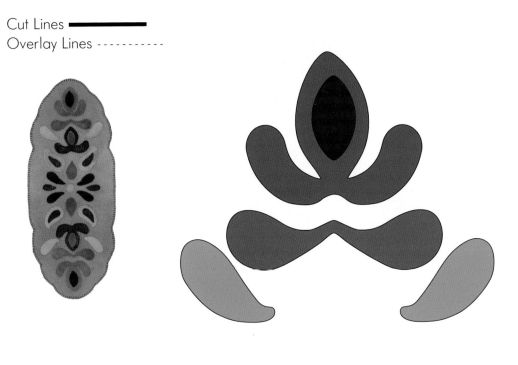

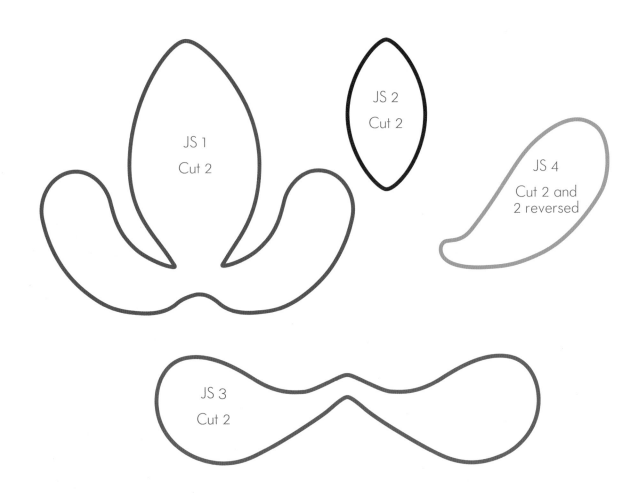

JS 1
Cut 2

JS 2
Cut 2

JS 4
Cut 2 and
2 reversed

JS 3
Cut 2

Cut Lines
---------- Overlay Lines

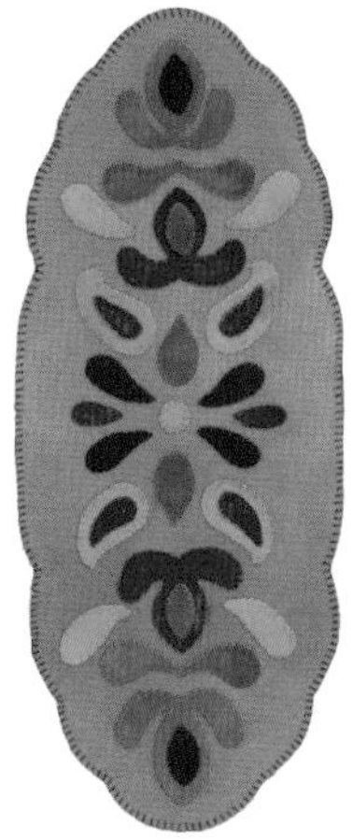

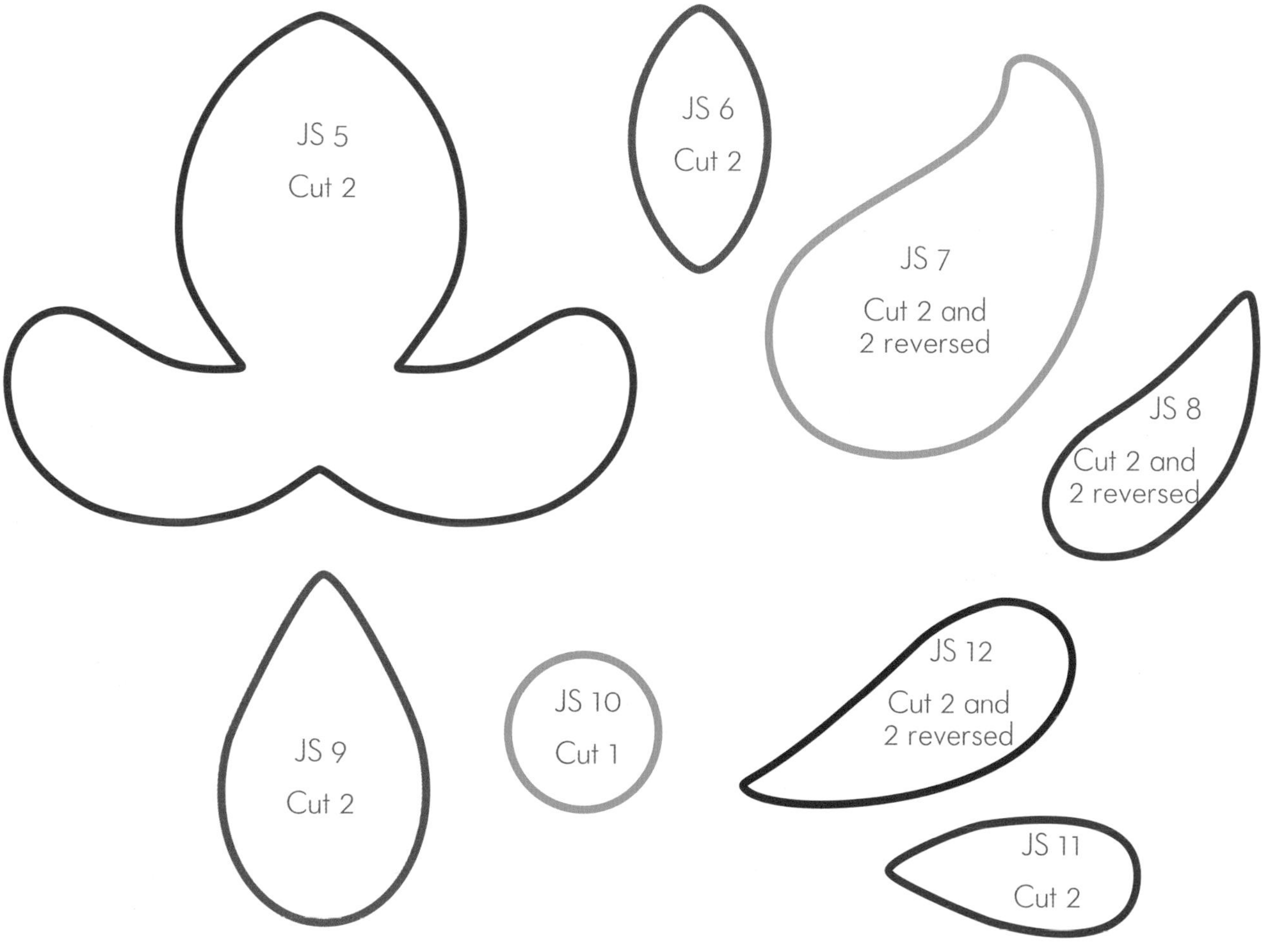

JS 5
Cut 2

JS 6
Cut 2

JS 7
Cut 2 and
2 reversed

JS 8
Cut 2 and
2 reversed

JS 9
Cut 2

JS 10
Cut 1

JS 12
Cut 2 and
2 reversed

JS 11
Cut 2

Kaleidoscope

A Wool Candle Mat

Finished Size: 10" x 15"

The arrangement of shapes creates a kaleidoscope of color for this lovely candle mat. Embellish the design by adding decorative embroidery stitches and beads.

Materials

Wool
Candle Mat Front: 12" x 16" rectangle
Candle Mat Back: 12" x 16" rectangle

Wool Appliqué
Turquoise: 12" square
Green: 8" square
Gold: 6" square
Raspberry: 6" square

Appliqué Patterns
Pages 32 and 34-35

Additional Materials
Freezer paper
Beads
Floss, perle cotton or wool threads
Chenille needle size 24
Embroidery needle size 10 for decorative stitching
Straw needle for bead embellishing
Fusible stabilizer (optional)

Refer to pages 6-12 before beginning the project.

Preparing the Appliqué

1. Using freezer paper and the template on page 32, cut out the candle mat front and back. Refer to page 8 for information on using freezer paper.

2. Using the shapes on pages 34-35 and referring to pages 8-10, prepare the appliqué shapes.

3. Place the shapes on the candle mat front referring to page 33 for placement.

4. Stitch the appliqué shapes to the candle mat front. Refer to pages 11-12 for stitching ideas.

5. Embellish the shapes with decorative stitches and beads.

Assembly Instructions

1. Layer and pin the candle mat front and back together.

2. Blanket stitch around the edges of the candle mat to secure the layers in place.

Cut Lines ▬▬▬
Overlay Lines ----------

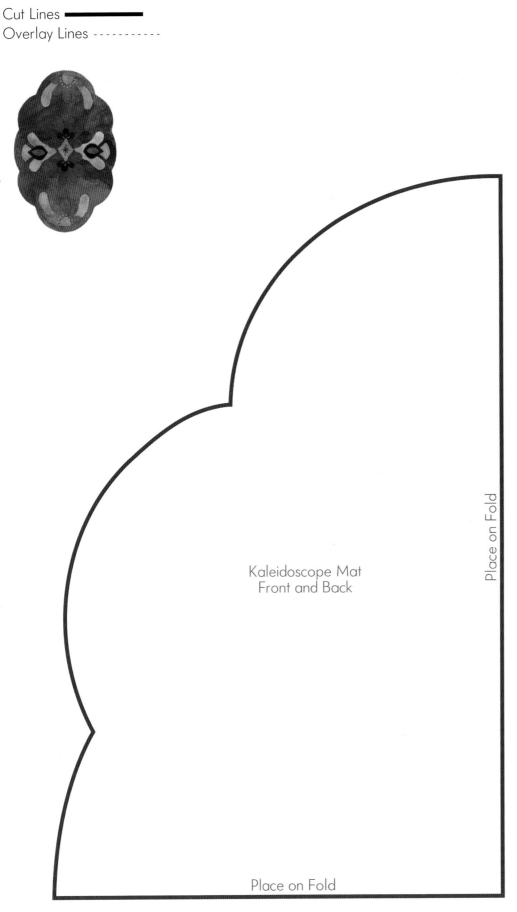

Kaleidoscope Mat
Front and Back

Place on Fold

Place on Fold

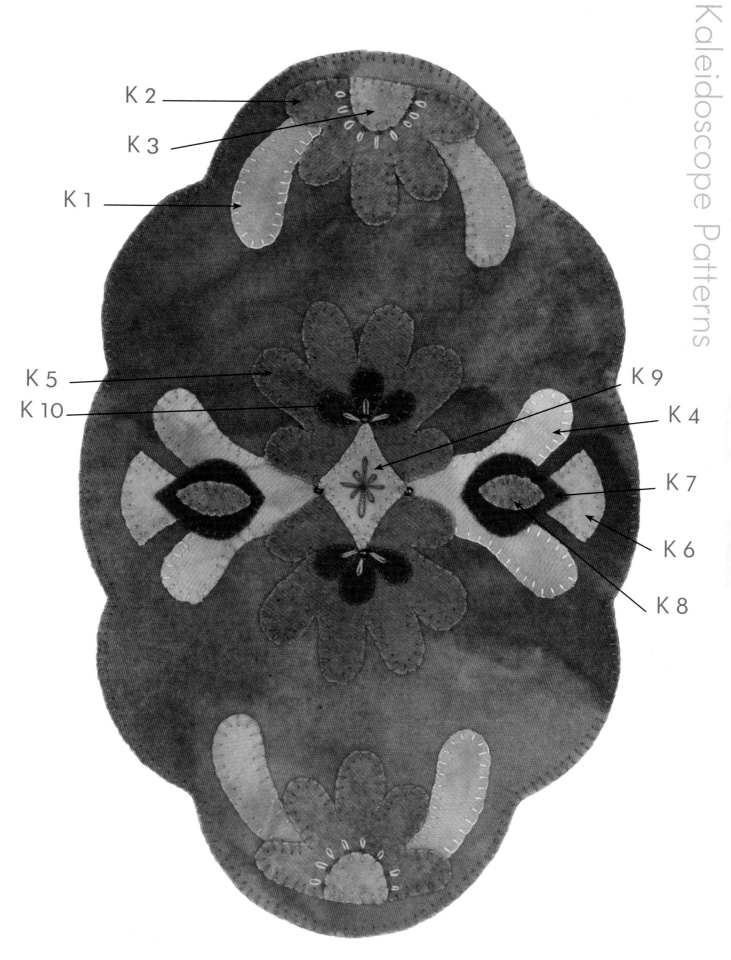

K 2

K 3

K 1

K 5

K 10

K 9

K 4

K 7

K 6

K 8

Cut Lines ━━━━━
Overlay Lines - - - - - - - - - -

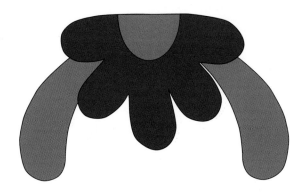

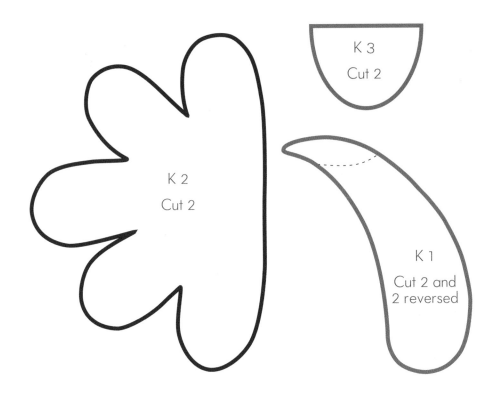

K 3
Cut 2

K 2
Cut 2

K 1
Cut 2 and
2 reversed

Cut Lines
Overlay Lines

K 5
Cut 2

K 10
Cut 6

K 9
Cut 1

K 4
Cut 2

K 7
Cut 2

K 6
Cut 2

K 8
Cul 2

Carousel of Circles

A Wool Table Runner

Finished Size: 18" x 48"

Dig into your wool stash to make this large table runner. It requires a wide assortment of colors, so it's a perfect stash-buster. The shapes are layered to create detailed circular units. These units can be stitched together individually and then sewn to the wool background fabric.

Materials

Wool

Table Runner Front: (1) 22" x 54" rectangle

Table Runner Back: (1) 22" x 54" rectangle

Wool Appliqué

Gold: 16" x 24" rectangle

Turquoise: 16" x 24" rectangle

Brown: 12" x 16" rectangle

Orange: 16" x 24" rectangle

Teal: 16" x 24" rectangle

Light Turquoise: 12" x 16" rectangle

Olive Green: 16" x 24" rectangle

Yellow Orange: 12" x 16" rectangle

Rust: 6" square

Dark Red: 12" x 16" rectangle

Peach: 12" x 16" rectangle

Beige: 6" square

Appliqué Patterns
Pages 38-46

Additional Materials
Floss, perle cotton or wool threads

Chenille needle size 24

Refer to pages 6-12 before beginning the project.

Cutting Instructions

From table runner front wool, cut:
   (1) 18" x 48" rectangle

From table runner back wool, cut:
   (1) 18" x 48" rectangle

Preparing the Appliqué

1. Using the shapes on pages 38-46 and referring to pages 8-10, prepare the appliqué shapes.

2. Using the photo on page 36 and the diagrams on page 47 as guides, layer and appliqué each individual circle unit. Refer to Layered Shapes on page 11.

3. Place the circle units on the table runner front following the photo on page 36.

4. Stitch the circle units to the table runner front. Refer to pages 11-12 for stitching ideas.

Assembly Instructions

1. Layer the appliquéd table runner front and table runner back together.

2. Blanket stitch around the edges of the table runner to secure the layers in place.

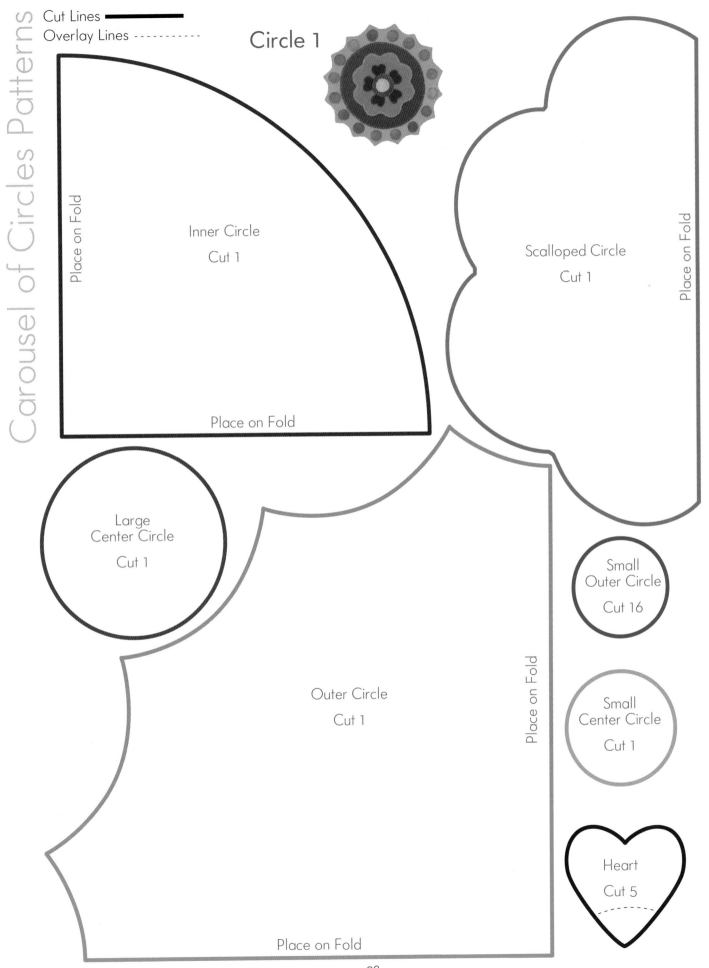

Carousel of Circles Patterns

Cut Lines ▬▬▬
Overlay Lines ----------

Circle 1

Place on Fold

Inner Circle
Cut 1

Place on Fold

Scalloped Circle
Cut 1

Place on Fold

Large
Center Circle
Cut 1

Small
Outer Circle
Cut 16

Outer Circle
Cut 1

Place on Fold

Small
Center Circle
Cut 1

Place on Fold

Heart
Cut 5

Circle 2

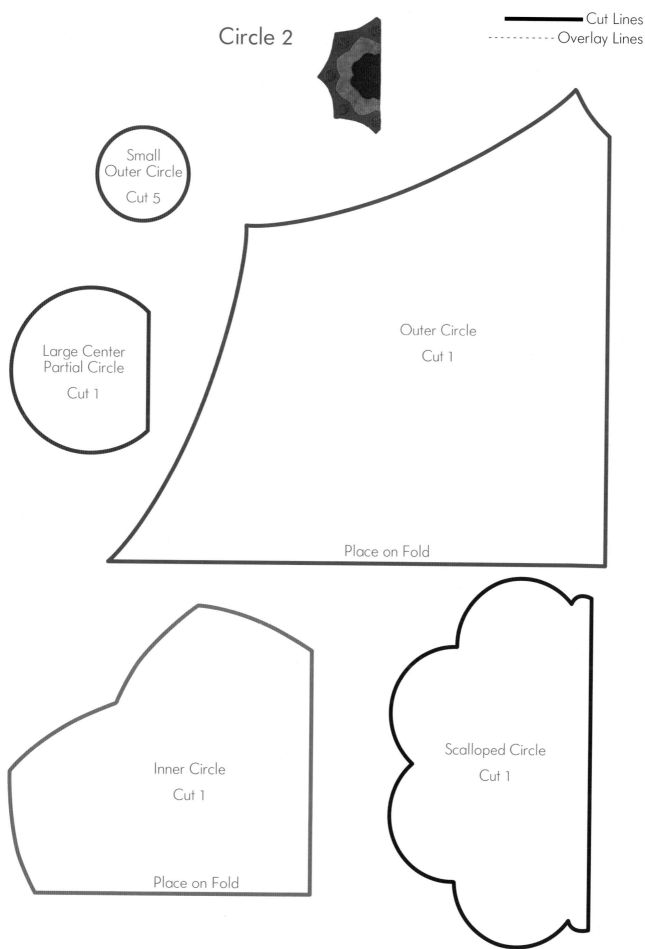

Cut Lines
Overlay Lines

Small
Outer Circle
Cut 5

Large Center
Partial Circle
Cut 1

Outer Circle
Cut 1

Place on Fold

Inner Circle
Cut 1

Place on Fold

Scalloped Circle
Cut 1

Cut Lines ━━━━━
Overlay Lines ----------

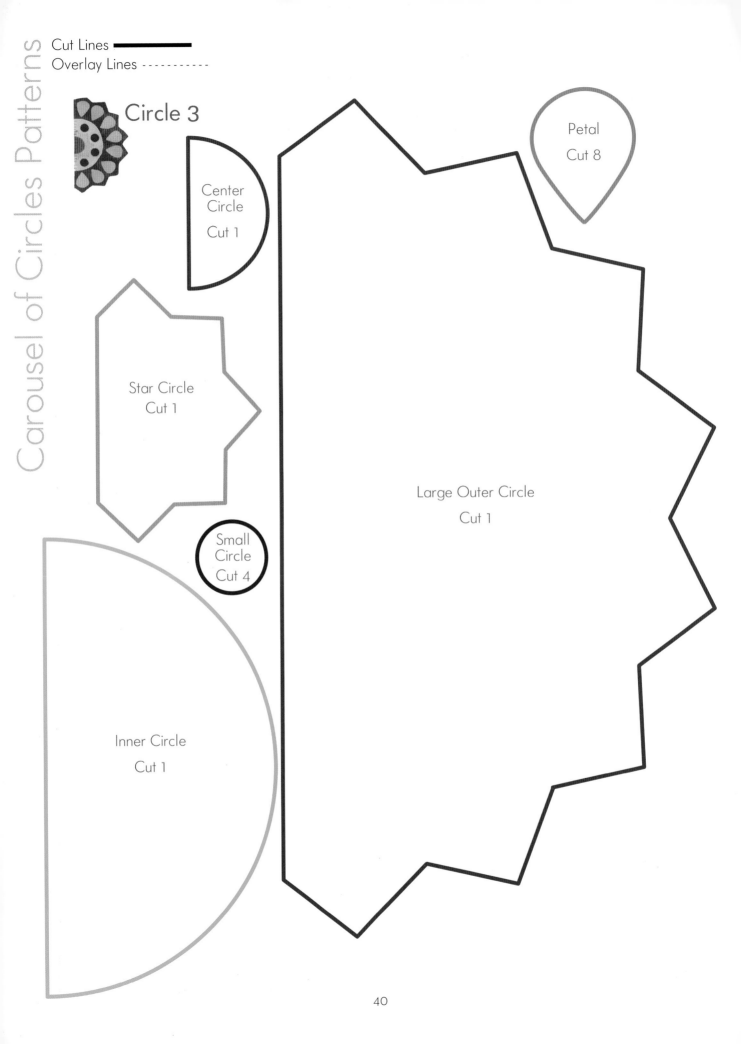

Circle 3

Center
Circle
Cut 1

Petal
Cut 8

Star Circle
Cut 1

Large Outer Circle
Cut 1

Small
Circle
Cut 4

Inner Circle
Cut 1

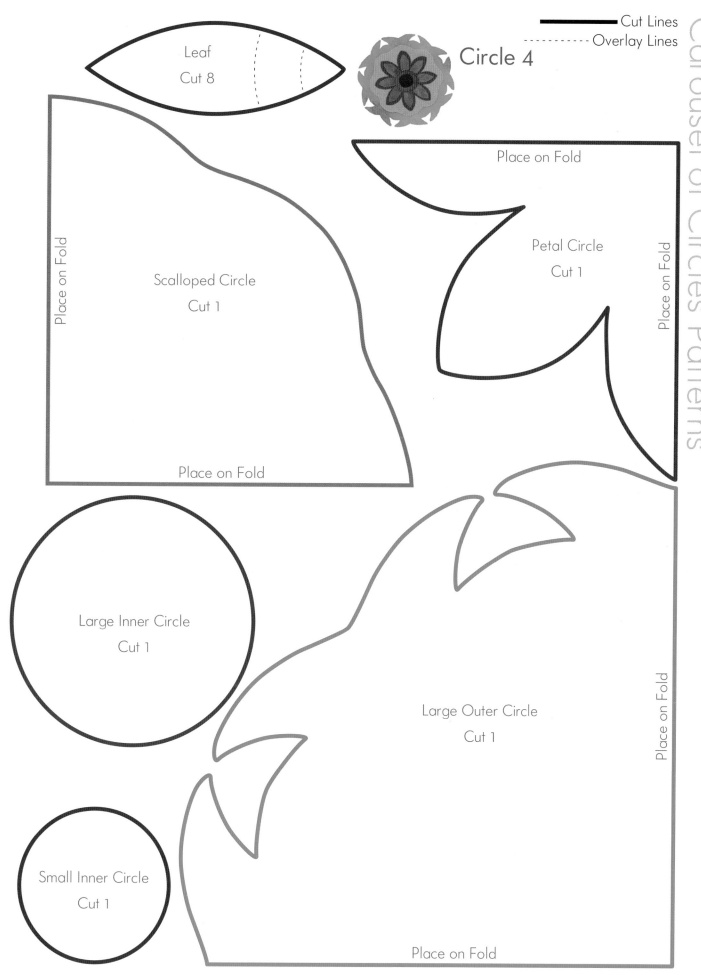

Cut Lines
Overlay Lines

Leaf
Cut 8

Circle 4

Place on Fold

Petal Circle
Cut 1

Place on Fold

Place on Fold

Scalloped Circle
Cut 1

Place on Fold

Large Inner Circle
Cut 1

Large Outer Circle
Cut 1

Place on Fold

Small Inner Circle
Cut 1

Place on Fold

Carousel of Circles Patterns

Cut Lines ▬▬▬▬▬
Overlay Lines - - - - - - - - -

Circle 5

Large
Center Circle
Cut 1

Small
Center Circle
Cut 1

Inner Petal
Cut 8

Outer Petal
Cut 16

Outer Circle
Cut 1

Place on Fold

Petal Circle
Cut 1

Place on Fold

42

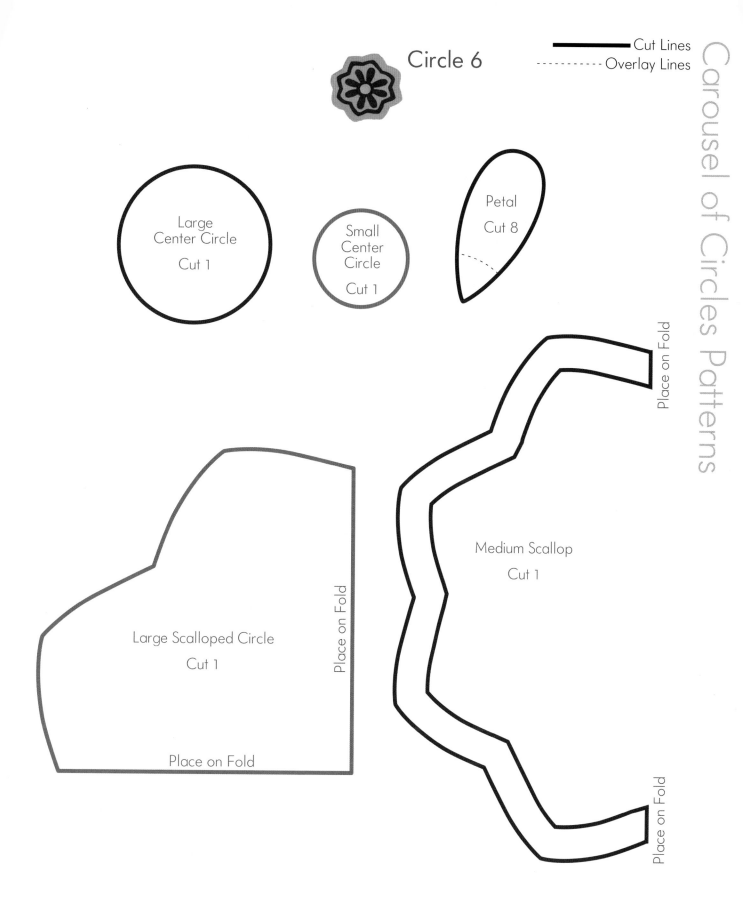

Circle 6

Cut Lines
Overlay Lines

Large
Center Circle
Cut 1

Small
Center
Circle
Cut 1

Petal
Cut 8

Place on Fold

Medium Scallop
Cut 1

Large Scalloped Circle
Cut 1

Place on Fold

Place on Fold

Place on Fold

Carousel of Circles Patterns

Cut Lines ▬▬▬
Overlay Lines ----------

Circle 7

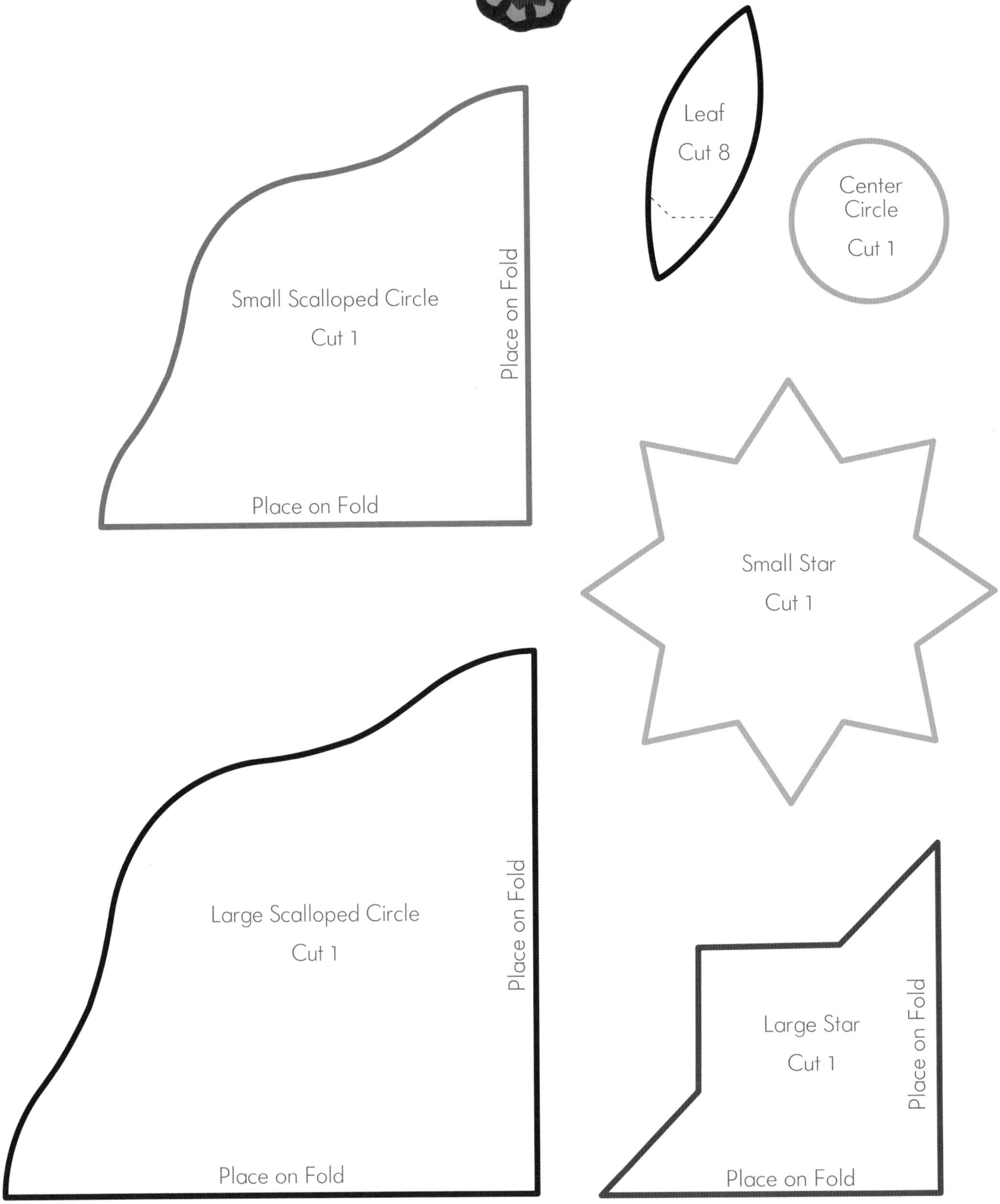

Leaf
Cut 8

Center
Circle
Cut 1

Small Scalloped Circle
Cut 1

Place on Fold

Place on Fold

Small Star
Cut 1

Large Scalloped Circle
Cut 1

Place on Fold

Place on Fold

Large Star
Cut 1

Place on Fold

Place on Fold

Circle 8

Cut Lines
Overlay Lines

Carousel of Circles Patterns

Place on Fold

Place on Fold

Small Scalloped Circle
Cut 1

Center
Circle
Cut 1

Puzzle Piece Circle
Cut 1

Place on Fold

Large Inner Circle
Cut 1

Place on Fold

Place on Fold

Place on Fold

Outer
Petal
Cut 16

Inner
Petal
Cut 5

Large Scalloped Circle
Cut 1

Place on Fold

Place on Fold

45

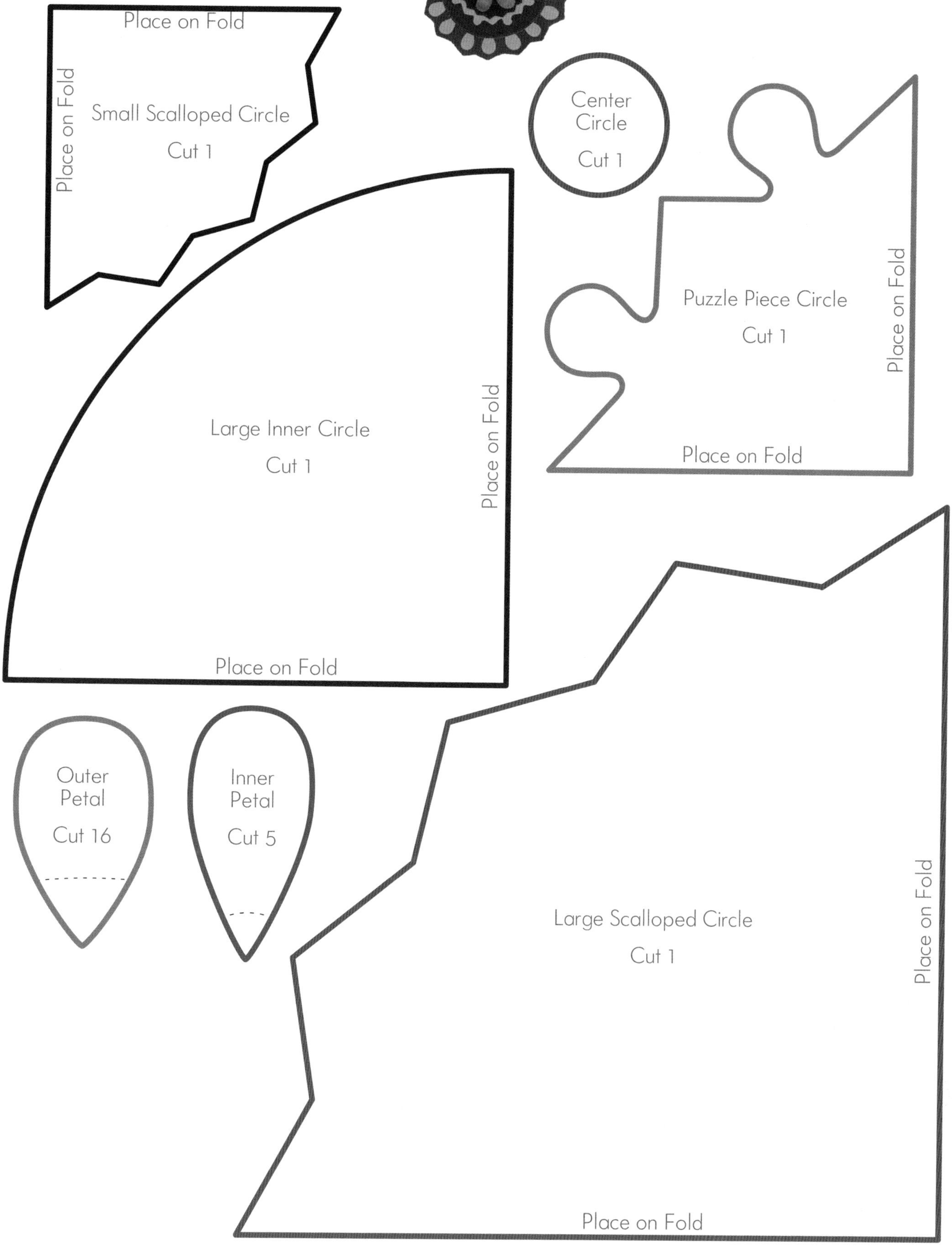

Cut Lines ▬▬▬
Overlay Lines ----------

Circle 9

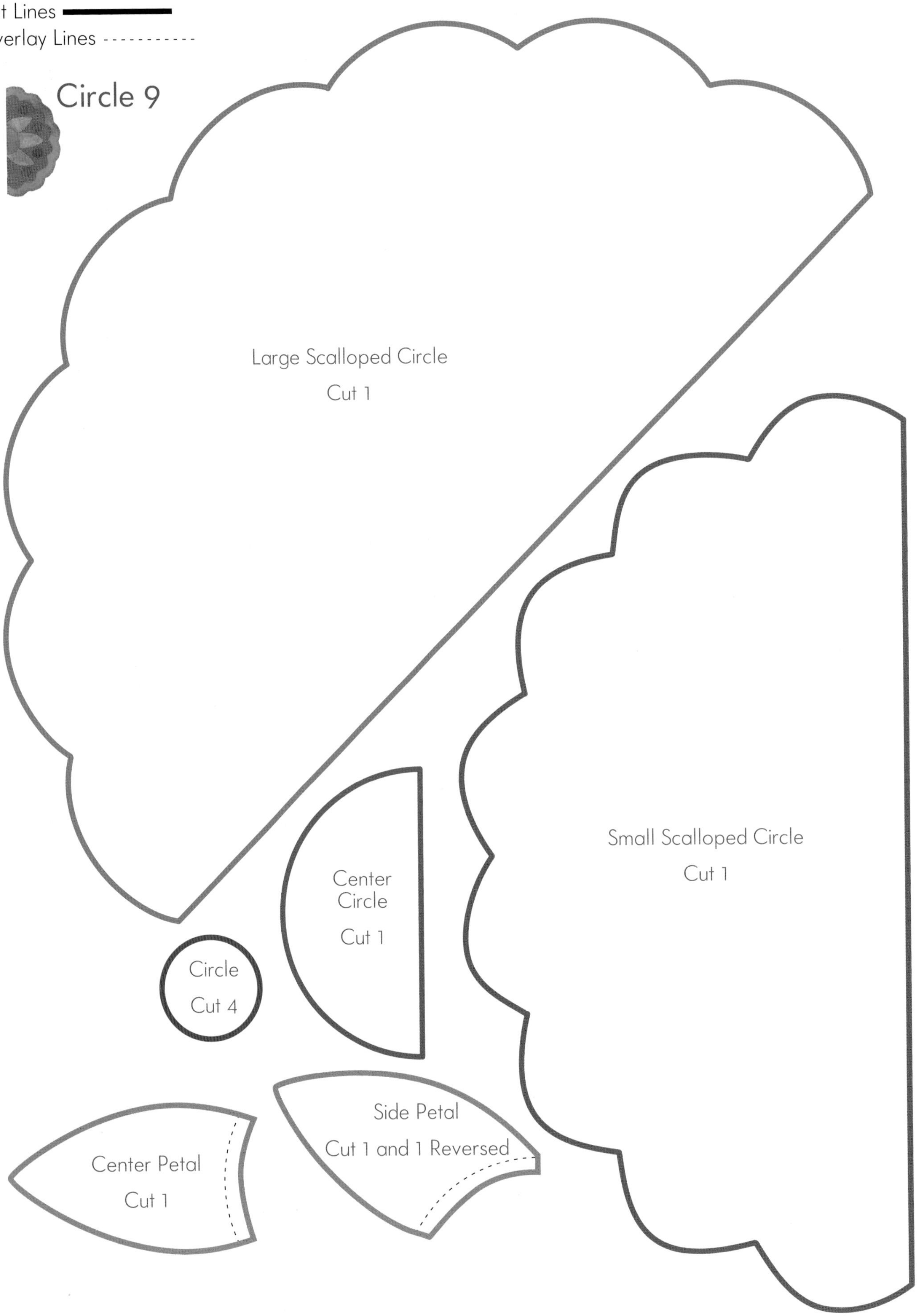

Large Scalloped Circle
Cut 1

Small Scalloped Circle
Cut 1

Center
Circle
Cut 1

Circle
Cut 4

Side Petal
Cut 1 and 1 Reversed

Center Petal
Cut 1

Cut Lines
Overlay Lines

Farmers' Market

A Wall Hanging

Finished Size: 24" x 30"

This nine-block wool appliqué wall hanging incorporates a variety of fun, simple shapes. Farmers' Market is a beginner project and the block size is easy to manipulate when hand-stitching. The featured wall hanging uses a flannel fabric for the background blocks, but a cotton background fabric would work as well.

Materials

Flannel or Cotton
Rust: 1/4 yard

Cream: 1/4 yard

Green: 1/4 yard

Gold: 1/4 yard

Backing: 1 yard

Binding: 1/3 yard

Wool Appliqué
Note: Choose your own colors or refer to the photo on page 48 for ideas.

Block 1
Pineapple: 6" square

Top and Base: 6" square:

Dots: 6" square

Block 2
Leaf: 8" square

Circles: 4" square

Branch: 5" x 7" rectangle

Block 3
Pomegranate: 8" square

Top: 4" square

Oval Center: 6" square

Inner Oval: 6" square

Dots: 4" square

Block 4
Heart: 6" square

Inner Heart: 6" square

Heart Bloom: 6" square

Leaf: 6" square

Circles: 4" square

Block 5
Flower: 6" square

Stem and Leaves: 6" square

Large and Small Ovals: 6" square

Block 6
Bird: 8" square

Crown: 2" square

Wing: 4" square

Beak and Legs: 3" square

Branch: 6" square

Leaves: 6" square

Eye: (2) 1" squares

Block 7
Large Flower: 6" square

Inner Flower: 4"square

Outer Flower: 4" square

Flower Base: 3" square

Stem: 4" square

Leaves: 4" square

Block 8
Outer Pear: 8" square

Large Inner Pear Shape: 6" square

Small Inner Pear Shapes: 3" square

Leaves: 4" square

Stem: 3" square

Block 9
Large Leaf: 6" square

Small Leaf: 3" square

Branch: 3" square

Inner Leaf: 6" square

Cornerstone Circles
(2) 4" squares

Appliqué Patterns
Pages 51-59

The appliqué shapes will need to be reversed if using a fusible product.

Additional Materials
Batting: 36" x 42" rectangle

Floss, perle cotton or wool threads

Chenille needle size 24

Basic sewing supplies

Refer to pages 6-12 before beginning the project.

wof = width of fabric

Cutting Instructions

From flannel or cotton fabrics, cut:
   (2) rust 8-1/2" x 10-1/2" rectangles
   (3) cream 8-1/2" x 10-1/2" rectangles
   (2) green 8-1/2" x 10-1/2" rectangles
   (2) gold 8-1/2" x 10-1/2" rectangles

From binding fabric, cut:
   (4) 2-1/2" x wof strips

From backing fabric, cut:
   (1) 35" x 40" rectangle

Preparing the Appliqué

1. Using the shapes on pages 51-59 and referring to pages 8-10, prepare the appliqué shapes.

2. Using the photos on pages 48 and 51-59 as guides, appliqué the shapes to the 8-1/2" x 10-1/2" flannel rectangles. Refer to Layered Shapes on page 11 and pages 11-12 for stitching ideas.

3. Using a stem stitch or other decorative stitch, embroider the vines on Block 8.

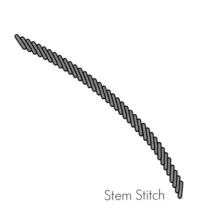

Stem Stitch

Assembly Instructions

1. Referring to the Wall Hanging Assembly Diagram, lay out the appliqué blocks in 3 rows with 3 blocks in each row.

2. Sew the blocks together in rows.

3. Sew the rows together to complete the wall hanging top.

Wall Hanging Assembly Diagram

Finishing the Wall Hanging

1. Layer the wall hanging top, batting and backing.

2. Hand-baste or pin the three layers together. Hand or machine quilt as desired.

3. Sew the (4) 2-1/2" x wof binding strips together to make one continuous strip.

4. Trim the extra batting and backing even with the edges of the wall hanging top.

5. Sew the binding to the edges of the wall hanging top.

6. Turn the binding over the edge to the back and hand- or machine-stitch in place.

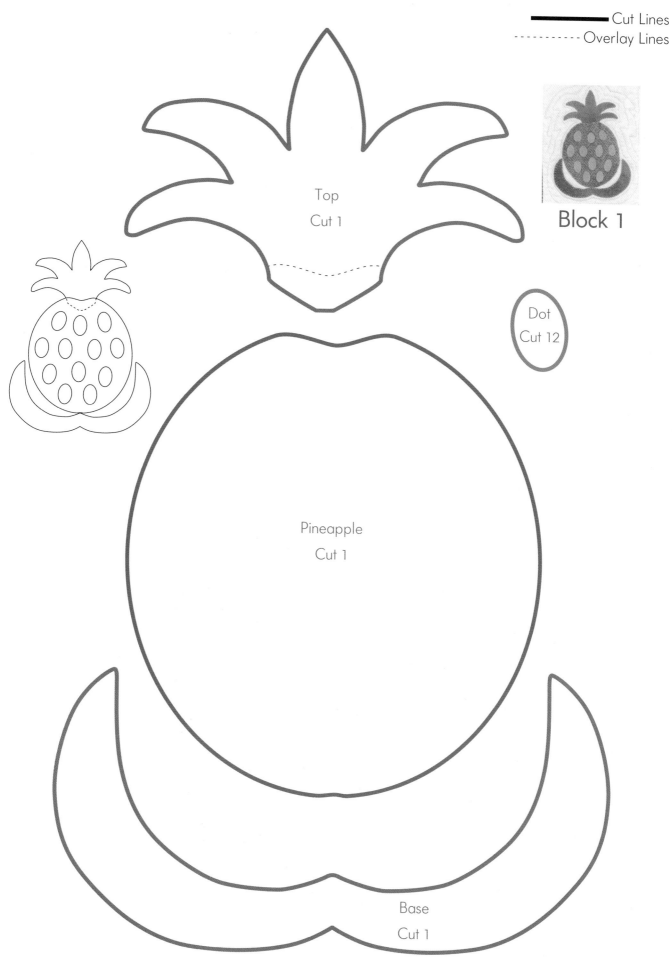

Cut Lines
Overlay Lines

Top
Cut 1

Block 1

Dot
Cut 12

Pineapple
Cut 1

Base
Cut 1

Cut Lines ━━━━━
Overlay Lines -----------

The appliqué shapes will need to be reversed if using a fusible product.

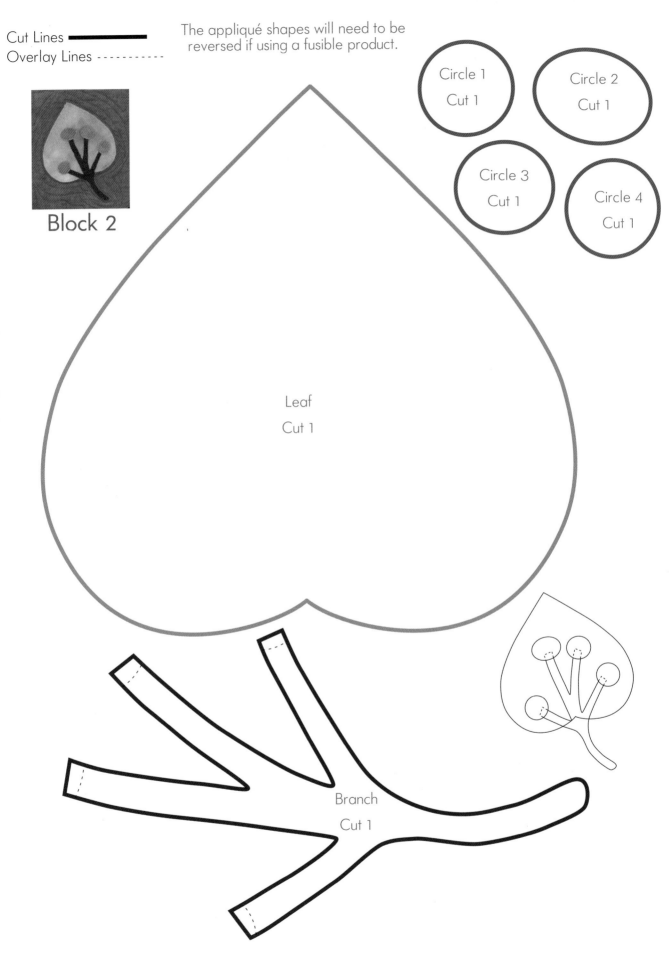

Block 2

Circle 1
Cut 1

Circle 2
Cut 1

Circle 3
Cut 1

Circle 4
Cut 1

Leaf
Cut 1

Branch
Cut 1

Cut Lines
Overlay Lines

Top
Cut 1

Inner Oval
Cut 1

Block 3

Dots
Cut 6

Pomegranate
Cut 1

Place on Fold

Oval Center
Cut 1

Cut Lines ▬▬▬▬
Overlay Lines ----------

Block 4

Heart Bloom
Cut 1

Circle
Cut 2

Heart
Cut 1

Inner Heart
Cut 1

Leaf
Cut 1

The appliqué shapes will need to be
reversed if using a fusible product.

━━━━━━━ Cut Lines
----------- Overlay Lines

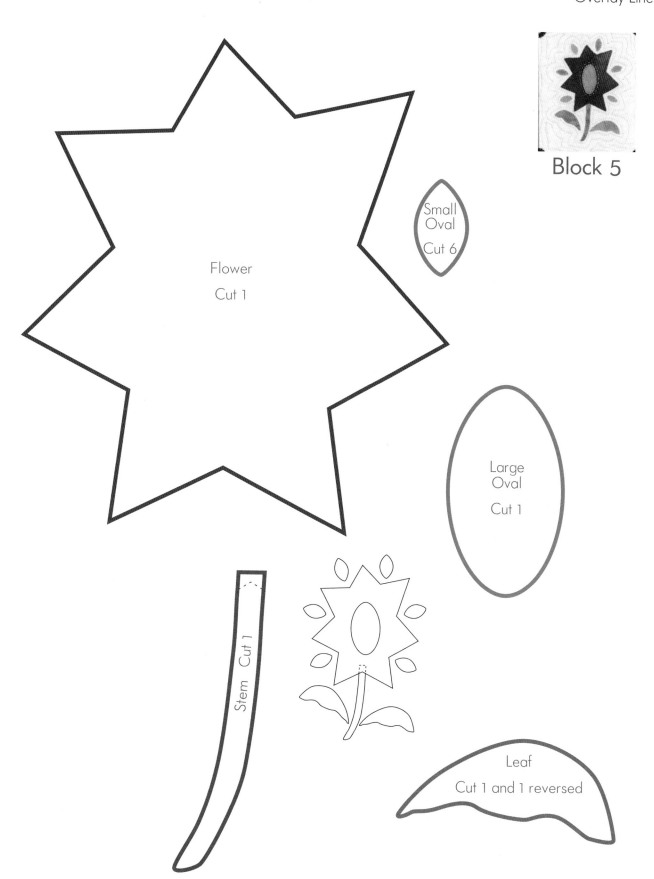

Block 5

Flower
Cut 1

Small
Oval
Cut 6

Large
Oval
Cut 1

Stem Cut 1

Leaf
Cut 1 and 1 reversed

Farmers' Market Patterns

Cut Lines ━━━
Overlay Lines ----------

The appliqué shapes will need to be
reversed if using a fusible product.

Block 6

Crown
Cut 1

Wing
Cut 1

Eye
Cut 1
of each

Bird
Cut 1

Beak
Cut 1

Leaf 1
Cut 1

Legs
Cut 1
of each

Leaf 2
Cut 1

Branch   Cut 1

Leaf 3
Cut 1

The appliqué shapes will need to be reversed if using a fusible product.

Cut Lines
Overlay Lines

Block 7

Large Flower
Cut 1

Outer Flower
Cut 1

Inner Flower
Cut 1

Flower Base
Cut 1

Leaf 1
Cut 1

Stem Cut 1

Leaf 2
Cut 1

Cut Lines ▬▬▬
Overlay Lines ----------

The appliqué shapes will need to be reversed if using a fusible product.

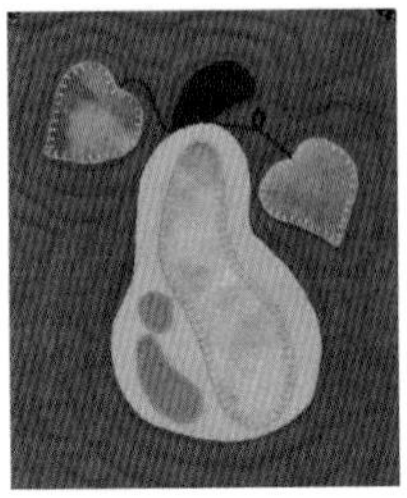

Farmers' Market Patterns

Block 8

Stem
Cut 1

Small
Inner
Pear 2

Cut 1

Leaf 2
Cut 1

Leaf 1
Cut 1

Small
Inner
Pear 1

Cut 1

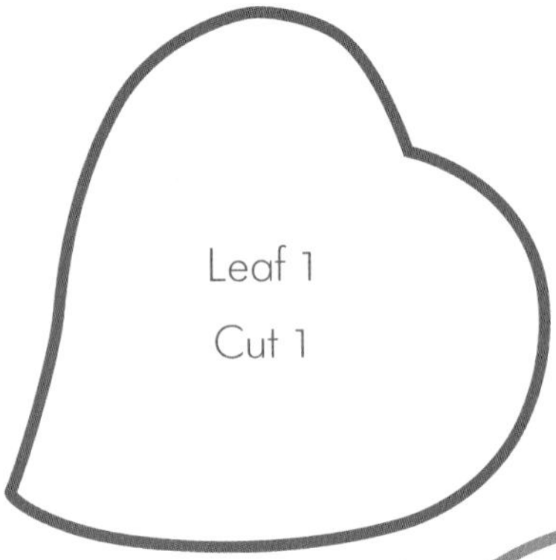

Large Inner Pear

Cut 1

Outer Pear

Cut 1

58

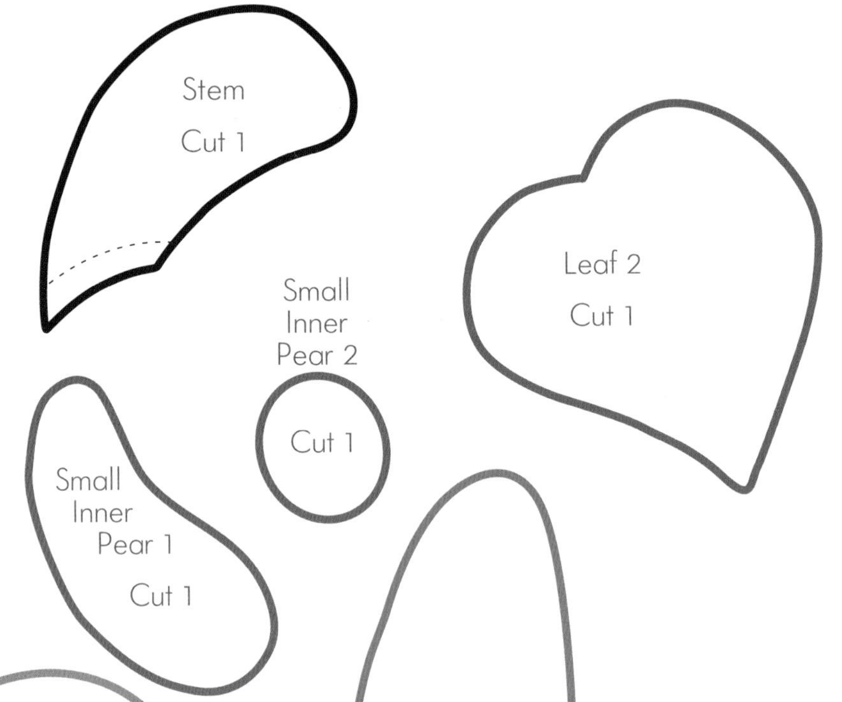

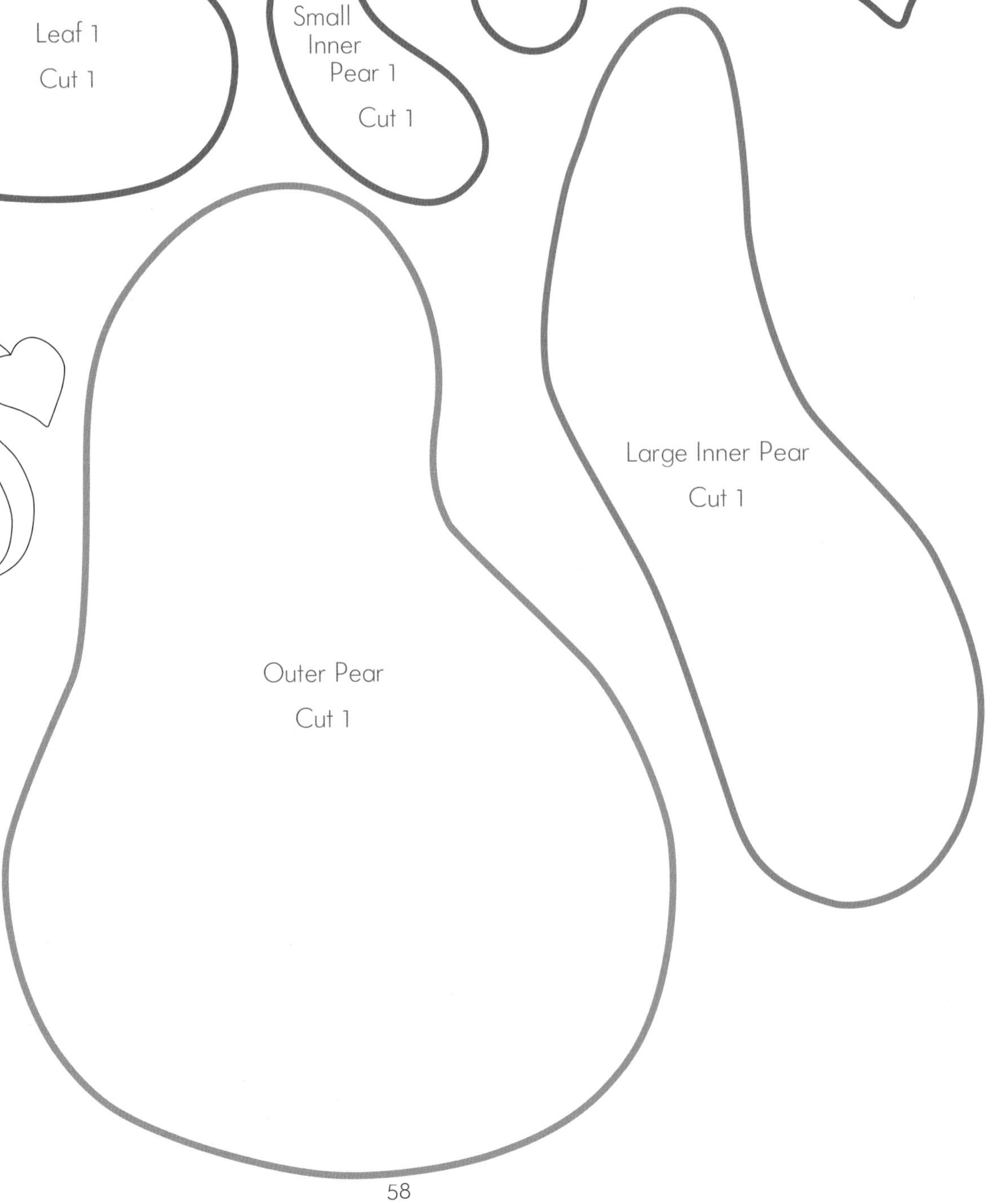

The appliqué shapes will need to be reversed if using a fusible product.

———— Cut Lines
- - - - - - - - Overlay Lines

Block 9

Large Leaf
Cut 1

Small Leaf
Cut 1

Inner Leaf
Cut 1

Branch
Cut 1

Large
Cornerstone
Cut 4

Cut 4

Small
Cornerstone

Autumn in the Woods

A Fall Table Runner

Finished Size: 13" x 30"

The unexpected colors used in this table runner, while not traditional fall colors, will brighten any autumn day. Autumn in the Woods would also be beautiful in realistic fall colors of red, orange, gold and brown.

Materials

Wool

Table Runner Front:
15" x 33" rectangle

Table Runner Back:
15" x 33" rectangle

Wool Appliqué

Tree Trunks:
12" x 16" dark brown rectangle

Leaves:
(1) 12" x 16" rectangle **each** of orange, red and lavender

Acorn Tops:
6" beige square

Acorn Bottoms:
6" brown square

Appliqué Patterns

Pages 62-63

Additional Materials

Floss, perle cotton or wool threads

Chenille needle size 24

Refer to pages 6-12 before beginning the project.

Cutting Instructions

From table runner front, cut:
  13" x 30" rectangle

From table runner back, cut:
  13" x 30" rectangle

Preparing the Appliqué

1. Using the shapes on pages 62-63 and referring to pages 8-10, prepare the appliqué shapes.

2. Place the shapes on the table runner front referring to photos on pages 60 and 62.

3. Stitch the shapes to the table runner front. Refer to pages 11-12 for stitching ideas.

Assembly Instructions

1. Layer the appliquéd table runner front and table runner back together.

2. Blanket stitch around the edges of the table runner to secure the layers in place.

Cut Lines ━━━━━━
Overlay Lines - - - - - - - - -

The appliqué shapes will need to be reversed if using a fusible product.

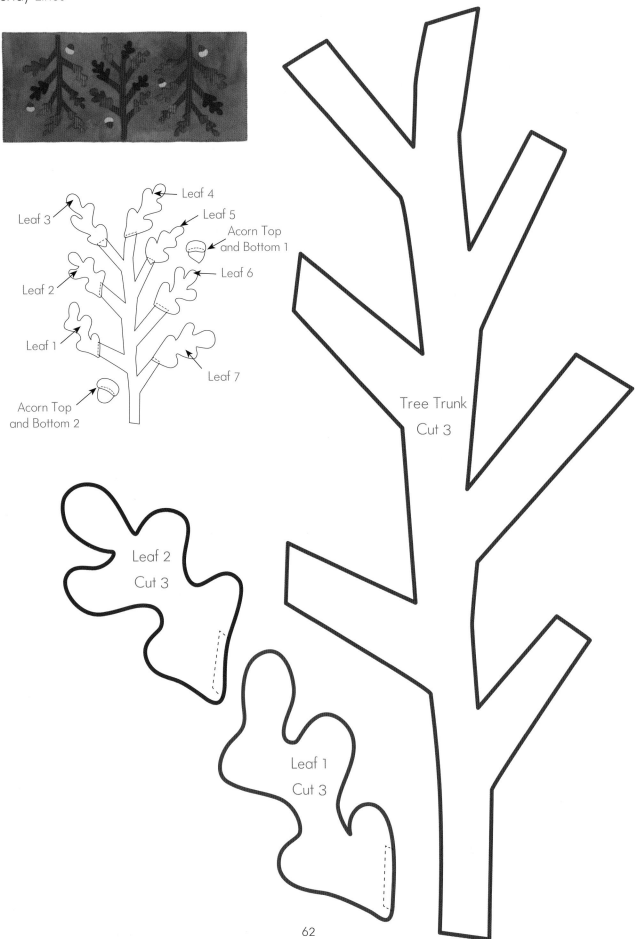

Leaf 4
Leaf 3
Leaf 5
Acorn Top and Bottom 1
Leaf 2
Leaf 6
Leaf 1
Leaf 7
Acorn Top and Bottom 2

Tree Trunk
Cut 3

Leaf 2
Cut 3

Leaf 1
Cut 3

The appliqué shapes will need to be reversed if using a fusible product.

——————— Cut Lines
- - - - - - - - Overlay Lines

Leaf 4
Cut 3

Acorn Top 1
Cut 3

Acorn
Bottom 1
Cut 3

Leaf 5
Cut 3

Leaf 3
Cut 3

Leaf 6
Cut 3

Acorn Top 2
Cut 3

Acorn
Bottom 2
Cut 3

Leaf 7
Cut 3

Trifecta

A Bell Pull

Finished Size: 8" x 27"

No one actually needs a bell pull, but everyone will love hanging this unique design. This beautiful project is all about the intricate stitching detail on the three appliqué blocks. Don't forget to add a tassel.

Materials

Wool
Bell Pull Front (Green): 9" x 32" rectangle

Block Backgrounds (Blue): 8" x 16" rectangle

Block Background (Purple): 8" square

Bell Pull Back: 9" x 32" rectangle

Wool Appliqué
White: 12" x 16" rectangle

Purple: 6" square

Blue: 6" square

Turquoise: 8" square

Orange-Gold: 6" square

Salmon: 4" square

Dark Gold: 4" square

Teal: 4" square

Green: 8" square

Appliqué Patterns
Pages 66-69

Additional Materials
Floss, perle cotton or wool threads

Assorted beads

Dowel or bell pull hanger

Tassel

Chenille needle size 24

Straw needle for bead embellishing

Embroidery needle size 10 for decorative stitching

Refer to pages 6-12 before beginning the project.

Cutting Instructions

From bell pull front wool, cut:
 (1) 8" x 29" rectangle

From block background wool, cut:
 (3) 7" squares

From bell pull back, cut:
 (1) 8" x 29" rectangle

Preparing the Appliqué

1. Using the shapes on pages 66-69 and referring to pages 8-10, prepare the appliqué shapes.

2. Referring to the photos on pages 64 and 67-69, position the shapes on the three background squares.

3. Stitch the shapes to the background squares. Refer to pages 11-12 for stitching ideas.

4. Embellish the shapes with decorative stitches and beads.

Note: Trifecta uses the following decorative stitches: Running, Chain, Feather and French Knots. Refer to page 12 for diagrams of the stitches.

5. Position tulip shapes on the bottom center of the bell pull front. These should be approximately 1/2" from the bottom edge. Stitch the shapes in place.

Cut Lines ▬▬▬▬
Overlay Lines ----------

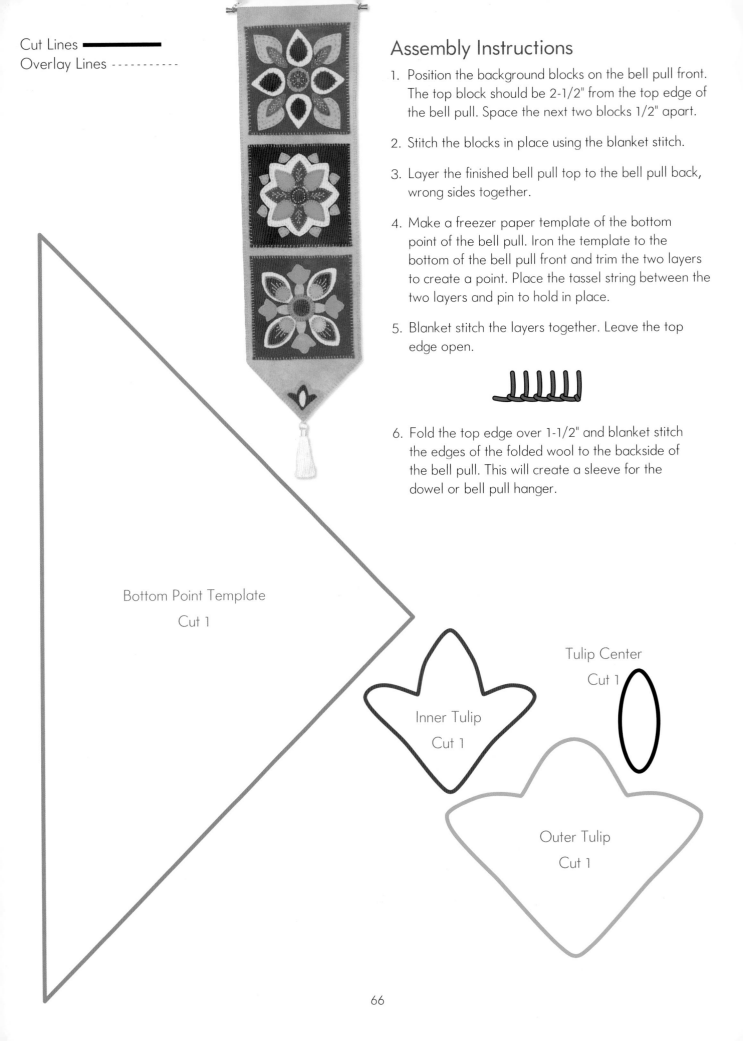

Assembly Instructions

1. Position the background blocks on the bell pull front. The top block should be 2-1/2" from the top edge of the bell pull. Space the next two blocks 1/2" apart.

2. Stitch the blocks in place using the blanket stitch.

3. Layer the finished bell pull top to the bell pull back, wrong sides together.

4. Make a freezer paper template of the bottom point of the bell pull. Iron the template to the bottom of the bell pull front and trim the two layers to create a point. Place the tassel string between the two layers and pin to hold in place.

5. Blanket stitch the layers together. Leave the top edge open.

6. Fold the top edge over 1-1/2" and blanket stitch the edges of the folded wool to the backside of the bell pull. This will create a sleeve for the dowel or bell pull hanger.

Bottom Point Template
Cut 1

Inner Tulip
Cut 1

Tulip Center
Cut 1

Outer Tulip
Cut 1

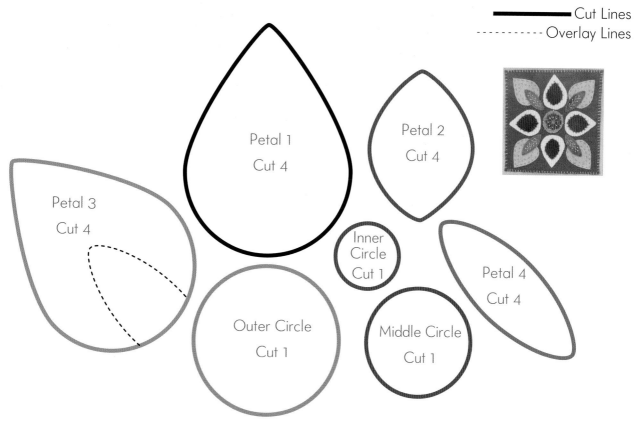

Cut Lines
Overlay Lines

Petal 1
Cut 4

Petal 2
Cut 4

Petal 3
Cut 4

Inner
Circle
Cut 1

Petal 4
Cut 4

Outer Circle
Cut 1

Middle Circle
Cut 1

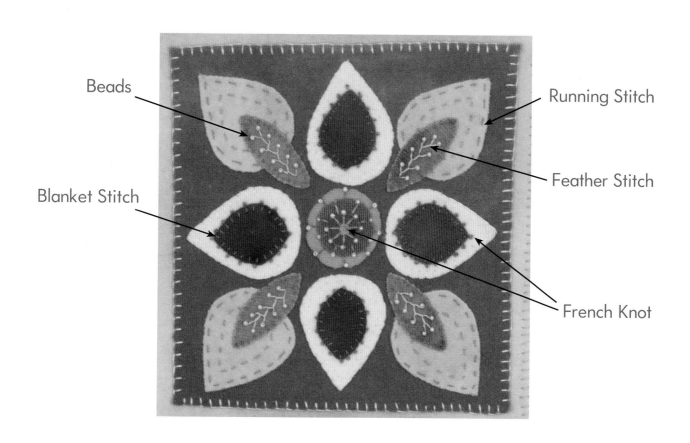

Beads

Running Stitch

Feather Stitch

Blanket Stitch

French Knot

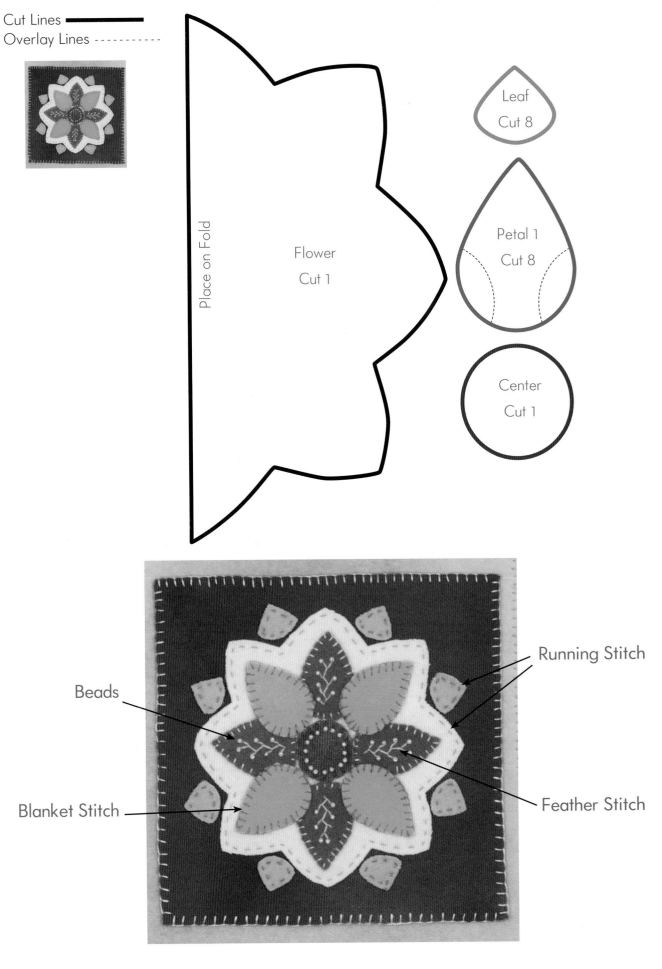

Cut Lines ——————
Overlay Lines - - - - - - - - - -

Place on Fold

Flower
Cut 1

Leaf
Cut 8

Petal 1
Cut 8

Center
Cut 1

Running Stitch

Beads

Feather Stitch

Blanket Stitch

Cut Lines
Overlay Lines

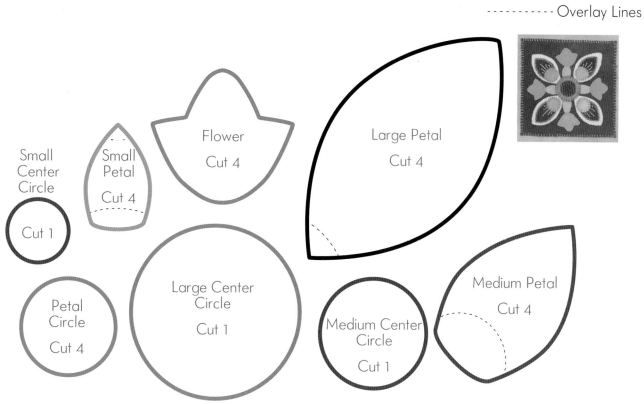

Small
Center
Circle

Cut 1

Small
Petal

Cut 4

Flower
Cut 4

Large Petal
Cut 4

Petal
Circle

Cut 4

Large Center
Circle

Cut 1

Medium Center
Circle

Cut 1

Medium Petal

Cut 4

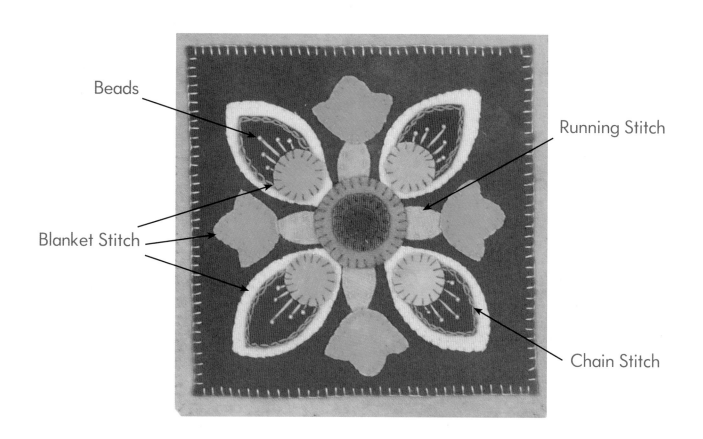

Beads

Running Stitch

Blanket Stitch

Chain Stitch

Bloomin' Paisley

A Decorative Pillow

Finished Size: 18" x 18"

Bright, colorful pillows with texture and pattern are popular home décor accessories. The wool appliqué block in the center front of the Bloomin' Paisley pillow is framed with a fun cotton border. The border fabric provides the color scheme for the pillow design.

Materials

Note: Choose your own colors or refer to the photo for ideas.

Cotton
Pillow Border: 1/4 yard

Flange: 1/8 yard

Wool
Pillow Center: 13" square

Pillow Back: 18-1/2" square

Wool Appliqué
Large Paisley: 6" x 8" rectangle

Scalloped Inner Paisley: 6" square

Small Inner Paisley: 6" square

Small Circle: 1-1/2" square

Large Leaves: 12" x 16" rectangle

Small Leaves: 3" square

Flower: 5" square

Flower Center: 2" square

Appliqué Patterns
Pages 73-75

The appliqué shapes will need to be reversed if using a fusible product.

Additional Materials
Pillow Form: 18" square

Assorted Beads

Floss, perle cotton or wool threads

Chenille needle size 24

Straw needle for bead embellishing

Refer to pages 6-12 before beginning project.

wof = width of fabric

Cutting Instructions

From pillow center wool, cut:
  (1) 12-1/2" square

From pillow border cotton, cut:
  (2) 3-1/2" x wof strips. From strips, cut:
    (2) 3-1/2" x 12-1/2" side border strips
    (2) 3-1/2" x 18-1/2" top/bottom border strips

From flange cotton, cut:
  (2) 1" x wof strips. From strips, cut:
    (4) 1" x 18-1/2" strips

Preparing the Appliqué

1. Using the shapes on pages 73-75 and referring to pages 8-10, prepare the appliqué shapes.

2. Referring to the photo, position the shapes on the pillow center wool square.

3. Stitch the shapes to the square to complete the pillow center. Refer to pages 11-12 and the photo for stitching ideas.

Assembly Instructions

1. Sew the side border strips to opposite sides of the pillow center.

2. Sew the top/bottom border strips to the top/bottom of the pillow center to complete the pillow top.

3. Fold the flange strips in half, wrong sides together, and press. Sew one flange strip to each side of the pillow top, aligning raw edges.

4. Layer the pillow front and pillow back, right sides together.

5. Using a 1/4" seam allowance, stitch around the outside to make the pillow cover. Leave a 10" opening along the bottom of the pillow cover.

6. Turn the pillow cover right side out.

7. Insert the pillow form into the pillow cover and hand-stitch the opening closed.

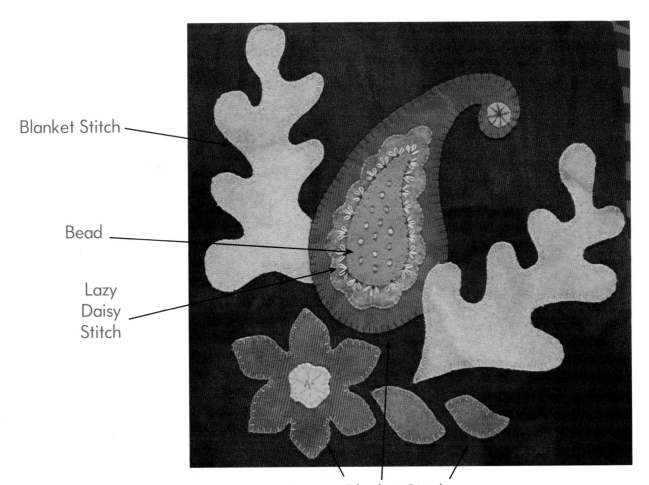

Blanket Stitch

Bead

Lazy Daisy Stitch

Blanket Stitch

The appliqué shapes will need to be reversed if using a fusible product.

Cut Lines
Overlay Lines

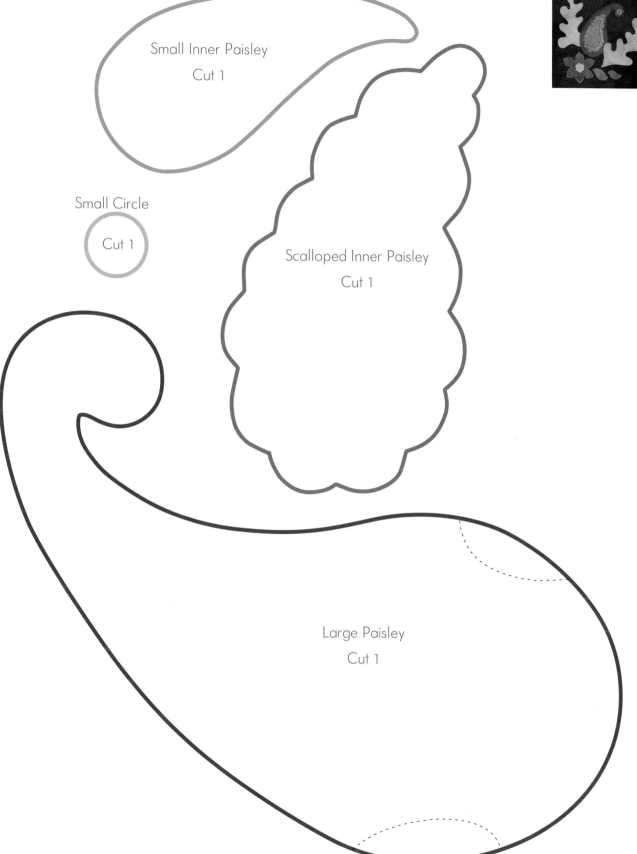

Small Inner Paisley
Cut 1

Small Circle

Cut 1

Scalloped Inner Paisley
Cut 1

Large Paisley

Cut 1

Cut Lines ━━━━━━━

Overlay Lines ---------

The appliqué shapes will need to be
reversed if using a fusible product.

Bloomin' Paisley Patterns

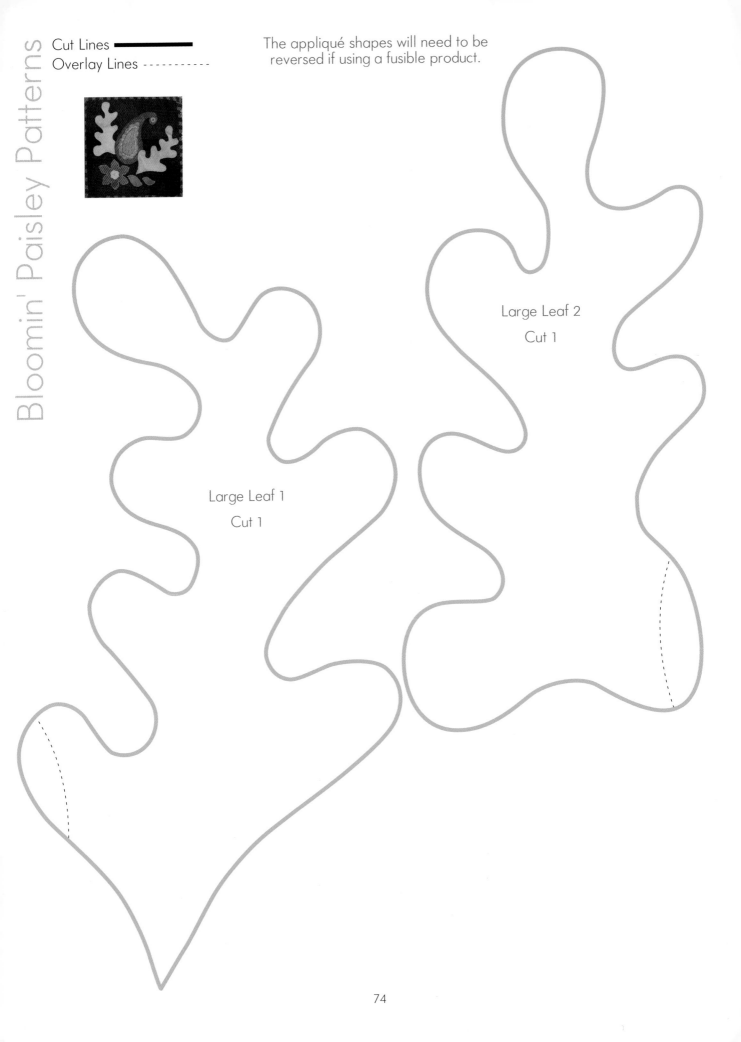

Large Leaf 2
Cut 1

Large Leaf 1
Cut 1

The appliqué shapes will need to be
reversed if using a fusible product.

————— Cut Lines
---------- Overlay Lines

Small
Leaf 1
Cut 1

Small Leaf 2
Cut 1

Flower
Center
Cut 1

Flower
Cut 1

ZigZag It

A Decorative Pillow

Finished Size: 11" x 22-1/2"

Begin with a dynamic cotton print for the ZigZag It pillow center and then add fun, colorful wool strips to each side. Buttons could be used in place of the wool circles.

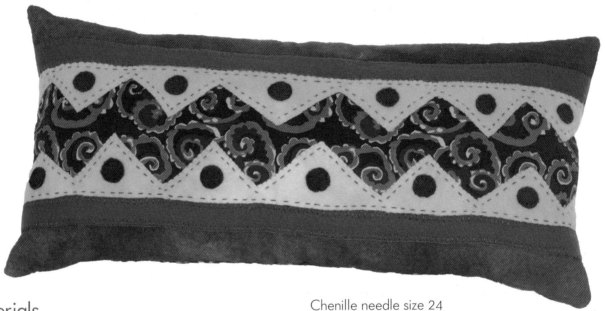

Materials
Note: Choose your own colors or refer to the photo for ideas.

Cotton
Pillow Center: 1/4 yard
Pillow Back: 3/8 yard

Wool
Pillow Front: 12" x 25" rectangle

Wool Appliqué
Narrow Strips: 4" x 25" rectangle
ZigZag Strips: 6" x 25" rectangle
Circles: 6" square

Appliqué Patterns
Pages 78-79

Additional Materials
Batting: 14" x 27" rectangle
Polyester Pillow Stuffing: 1 Bag
Floss, perle cotton or wool threads

Chenille needle size 24
Embroidery needle size 10

Refer to pages 6-12 before beginning the project.

Cutting Instructions
From pillow front wool, cut:
  (1) 11-1/2" x 23" rectangle

From pillow center cotton, cut:
  (1) 5" x 23" rectangle

From narrow strips wool, cut:
  (2) 1" x 23" strips

Preparing the Appliqué
Using the shapes on pages 78-79 and referring to pages 8-10, prepare the appliqué shapes.

Assembly Instructions

1. Position the cotton pillow center strip in the middle of the wool pillow front.

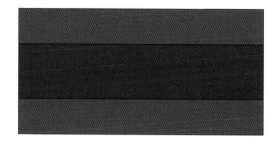

2. Baste the strip in place. Do not turn under raw edges.

3. Position the zigzag strips over the center strip. Secure with pins or a hand basting stitch. Stitch the zigzag strips in place using a decorative running stitch. See the diagram on page 12.

4. Position the narrow wool strips on either side of the zigzag strips and blanket stitch in place. The narrow strips butt up against the zigzag strips. Do not overlap them.

5. Position the wool circles on the zigzag strips. Stitch the circles in place to complete the pillow top.

6. Layer the cotton pillow back and batting. Machine quilt the layers.

7. Trim the pillow back to 11-1/2" x 23".

8. Layer the pillow front and back, right sides together. Using a 1/4" seam allowance, stitch around the outside to make the pillow cover. Leave an 8" opening along the bottom of the pillow cover.

9. Turn the pillow cover right side out.

10. Insert the pillow stuffing. Make sure to add extra stuffing to fill in the corners of the pillow.

11. Hand-stitch the opening closed.

ZigZag It Patterns

Cut Lines ▬▬▬▬
Seam Lines --------

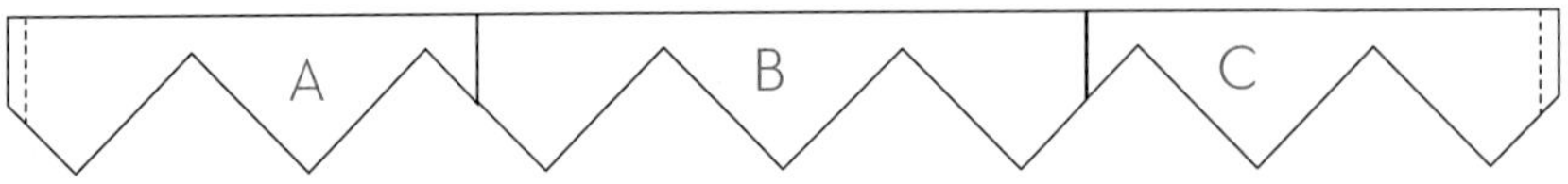

A   B   C

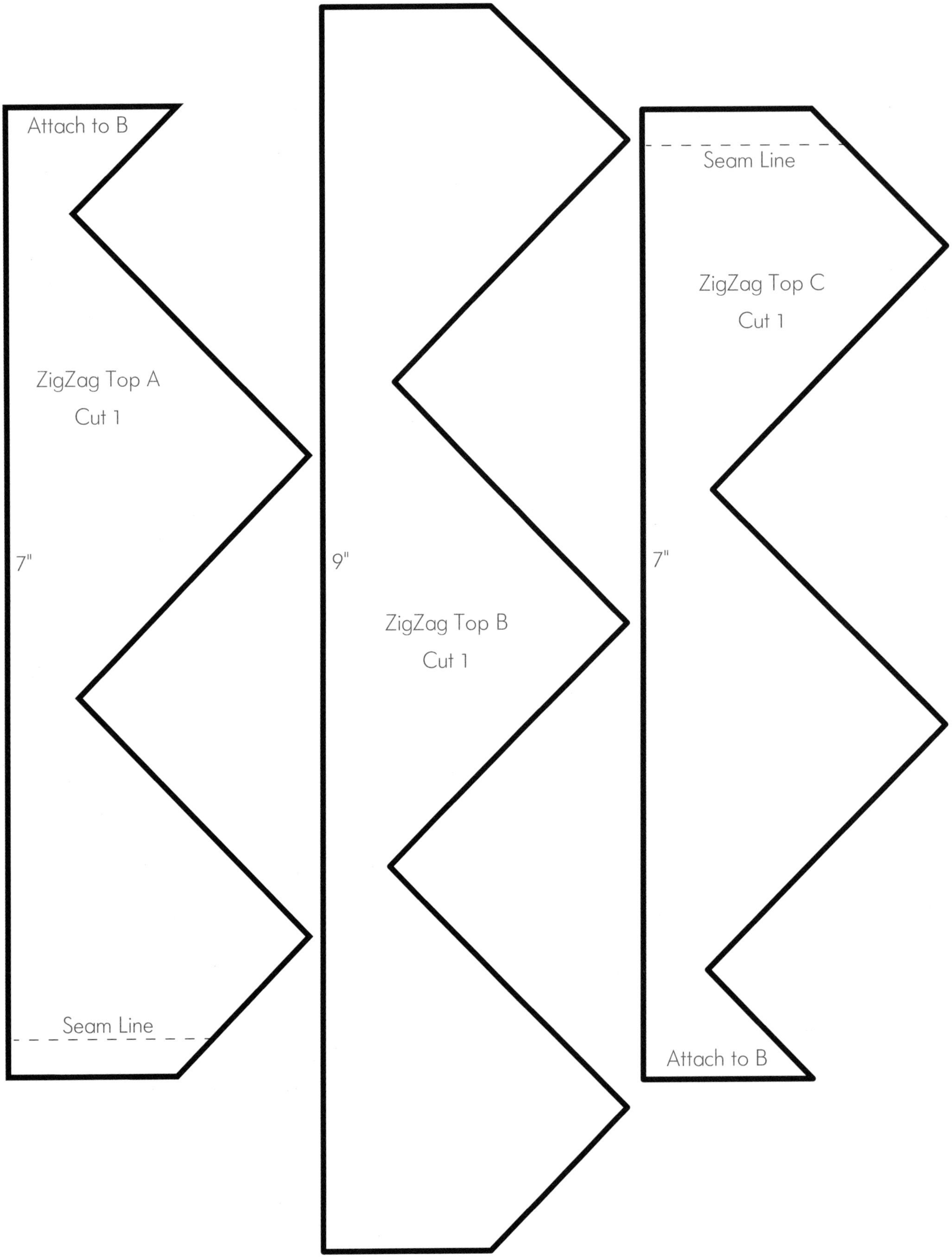

Attach to B

ZigZag Top A
Cut 1

7"

Seam Line

ZigZag Top B
Cut 1

9"

ZigZag Top C
Cut 1

Seam Line

7"

Attach to B

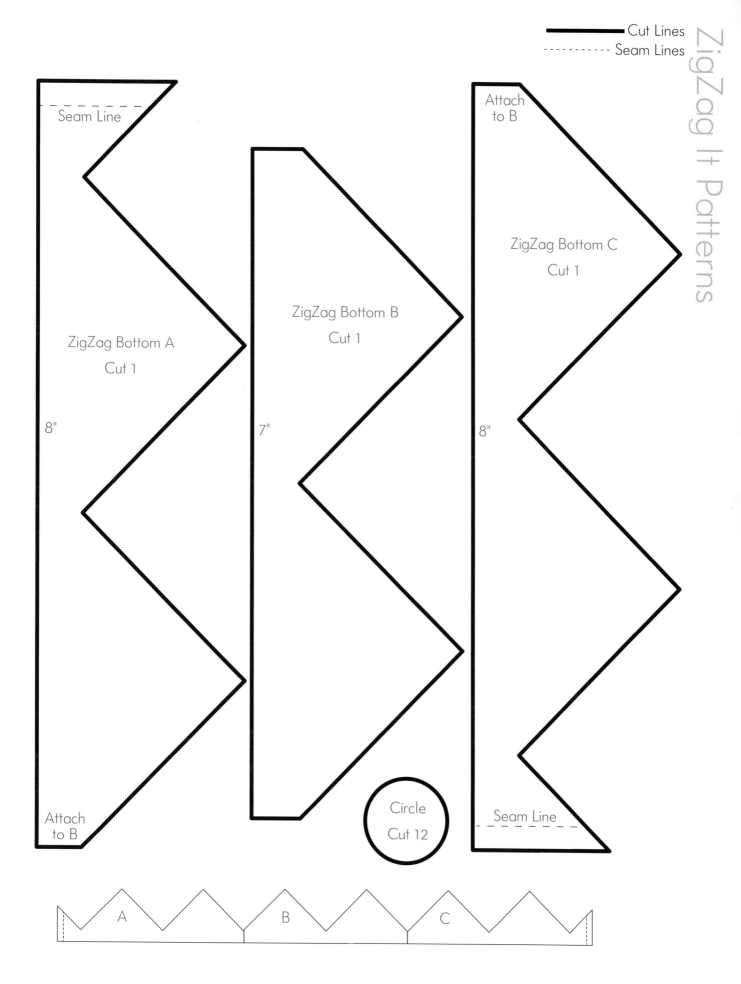

Cut Lines
Seam Lines

Seam Line

Attach
to B

ZigZag Bottom C
Cut 1

ZigZag Bottom A
Cut 1

ZigZag Bottom B
Cut 1

8"

7"

8"

Attach
to B

Circle
Cut 12

Seam Line

Attach
to B

A   B   C

Quartered Blossoms

A Decorative Pillow

Finished Size: 18" x 18"

The Quartered Blossoms pillow design resembles a large Mediterranean tile. Complete the four wool scalloped triangle units before stitching them to the pillow front.

Materials

Note: Choose your own colors or refer to the photo for ideas.

Cotton
Pillow Front: 5/8 yard
Pillow Back: 5/8 yard

Wool Appliqué
Scalloped Triangles and Trim: (2) 10" x 30" rectangle
Flower Halves: 10" x 12" rectangle
Flower Circles: 6" square
Center Shapes: 6" square
Oval Centers: 4" square

Appliqué Patterns
Pages 81-83

Additional Materials
Batting: 20" square
Pillow Form: 18" square
Floss, perle cotton or wool threads
Chenille needle size 24

Refer to pages 6-12 before beginning the project.

Cutting Instructions

From pillow front cotton, cut:
(1) 18-1/2" square

From pillow back cotton, cut:
(1) 20" square

Preparing the Appliqué

1. Using the shapes on pages 81-83 and referring to pages 8-10, prepare the appliqué shapes.

2. Referring to the photo on page 80, place the shapes on the scalloped triangles. Do not place and stitch the center shapes and oval centers yet.

3. Stitch the shapes to the scalloped triangles. Refer to pages 11-12 for stitching ideas.

4. Position and stitch the scalloped triangles to the pillow front.

5. Position and stitch the center shapes and oval centers to complete the pillow front.

Assembly Instructions

1. Layer the cotton pillow back and batting. Machine quilt the layers. Trim the layers to 18-1/2" square.

2. Layer the pillow front and back, right sides together. Using a 1/4" seam allowance, stitch around the outside to make the pillow cover. Leave a 10" opening along the bottom of the pillow cover.

3. Turn the pillow cover right side out.

4. Insert the pillow form into the pillow cover and hand stitch the opening closed.

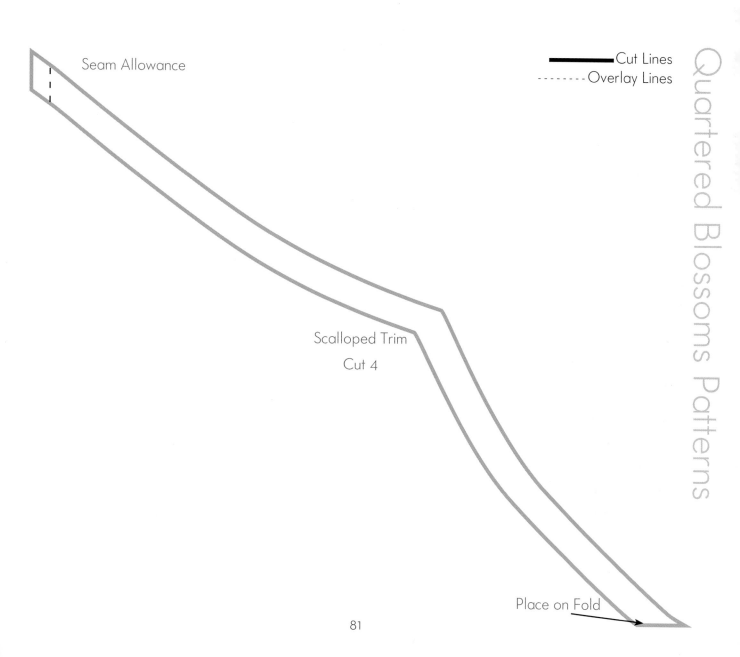

Seam Allowance

━━━━Cut Lines
- - - - - - - Overlay Lines

Scalloped Trim

Cut 4

Place on Fold

Quartered Blossoms Patterns

Cut Lines ━━━━━

Overlay Lines ----------

Oval
Center   Cut 4

Center Shape

Cut 4

Flower Circle

Cut 4

Flower Half

Cut 4

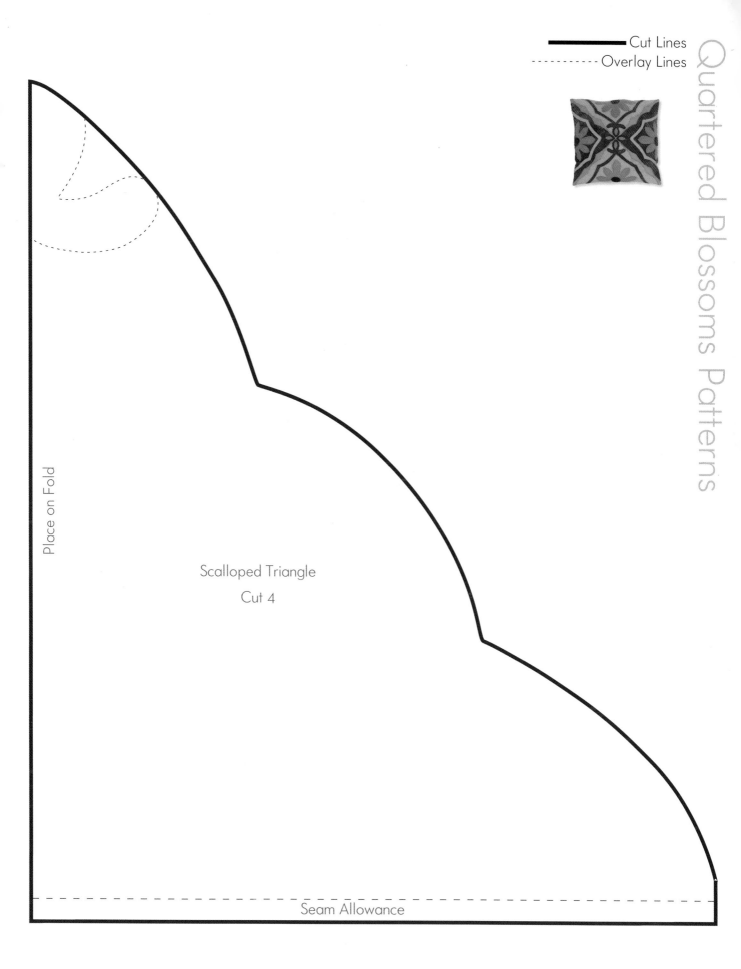

Cut Lines
Overlay Lines

Place on Fold

Scalloped Triangle

Cut 4

Seam Allowance

Puttin' on the Paisley

A Decorative Pillow

Finished Size: 15" x 20"

The silk background fabric gives the Puttin' on the Paisley pillow a royal look. Different types of fabrics with a variety of textures will create interesting paisleys. Cotton or silk could be layered to enhance each shape. Decorative stitches and beads were used to embellish the paisleys. A funky trim adds the final touch.

Note: I enjoy stitching on silk, but it tends to ravel easily. To eliminate this problem, over-size the background and trim to the unfinished size after the appliqué work is complete. Use a zigzag stitch or serge along the edge of the silk background to stop any fraying. A lightweight woven fusible stabilizer can also be ironed to the back of the silk to provide added structure.

Materials

Note: Choose your own colors or refer to the photo for ideas.

Silk

Pillow Front: 1/2 yard

Small Paisleys: Variety of small pieces or (4) 6" squares
Note: these can be a combination of silk, cotton and wool

Cotton

Pillow Back: 1/2 yard

Wool Appliqué

Paisleys: (7) 12" x 16" rectangles

Appliqué Patterns

Pages 86-95

The appliqué shapes will need to be reversed if using a fusible product.

Additional Materials

Batting: 18" x 24" rectangle

Fringe: 2-1/4 yards

Floss, perle cotton or wool thread

Assorted beads

Woven fusible stabilizer (optional): 1/2 yard

Polyester pillow stuffing: 1 bag

Chenille needle size 24

Straw needle for embellishing

Refer to pages 6-12 before beginning project.

Cutting Instructions

From pillow front silk, cut:
  (1) 16" x 22" rectangle

From pillow back cotton, cut:
  (1) 16" x 22" rectangle

From woven fusible stabilizer (if using), cut:
  (1) 16" x 22" rectangle

Preparing the Appliqué

1. Using the shapes on pages 86-95 and referring to pages 8-10, prepare the appliqué shapes. Note: If using silk for the small paisleys, refer to fusing instructions on pages 9-10.

2. Referring to the photo on page 84 and the placement diagram, position the shapes on the pillow front.

3. Stitch the shapes to the front to complete the pillow top. Refer to pages 11-12 for stitching ideas.

Assembly Instructions

1. Trim the pillow top to 15-1/2" x 20-1/2".

2. Layer the cotton pillow back and batting. Machine quilt the layers.

3. Trim the pillow back to 15-1/2" x 20-1/2".

4. Stitch the fringe to the right side of the pillow front. The fringe edge will be to the inside of the pillow top. The edge of the trim should align with the outer edge of the pillow top.

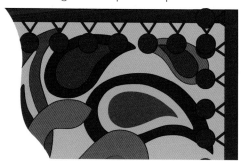

5. Layer the pillow front and back, right sides together. Stitch around the edge of the layers using a 1/4"-1/2" seam allowance. Leave a 10" opening along the bottom of the pillow cover.

6. Turn the pillow cover right side out.

7. Insert the pillow stuffing. Make sure to add extra stuffing to fill in the corners of the pillow.

8. Hand-stitch the opening closed.

Numbering Schematic

Placement Diagram

Note: Each paisley shape is labeled with a number. The number does not indicate order of placement. Refer to the photo on page 84 for placement.

Cut Lines ━━━━━━
Overlay Lines ----------

The appliqué shapes will need to be
reversed if using a fusible product.

Paisley 1

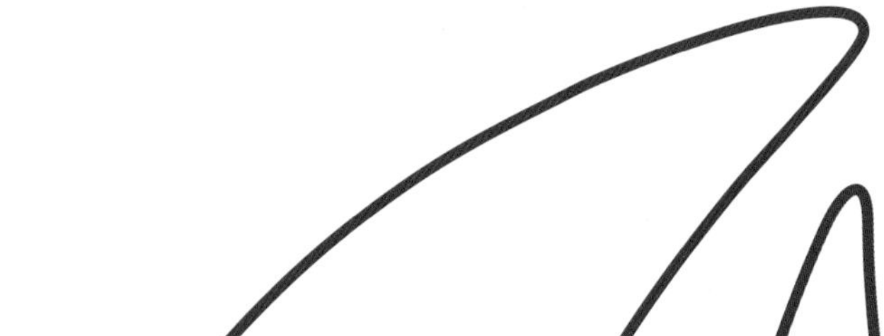

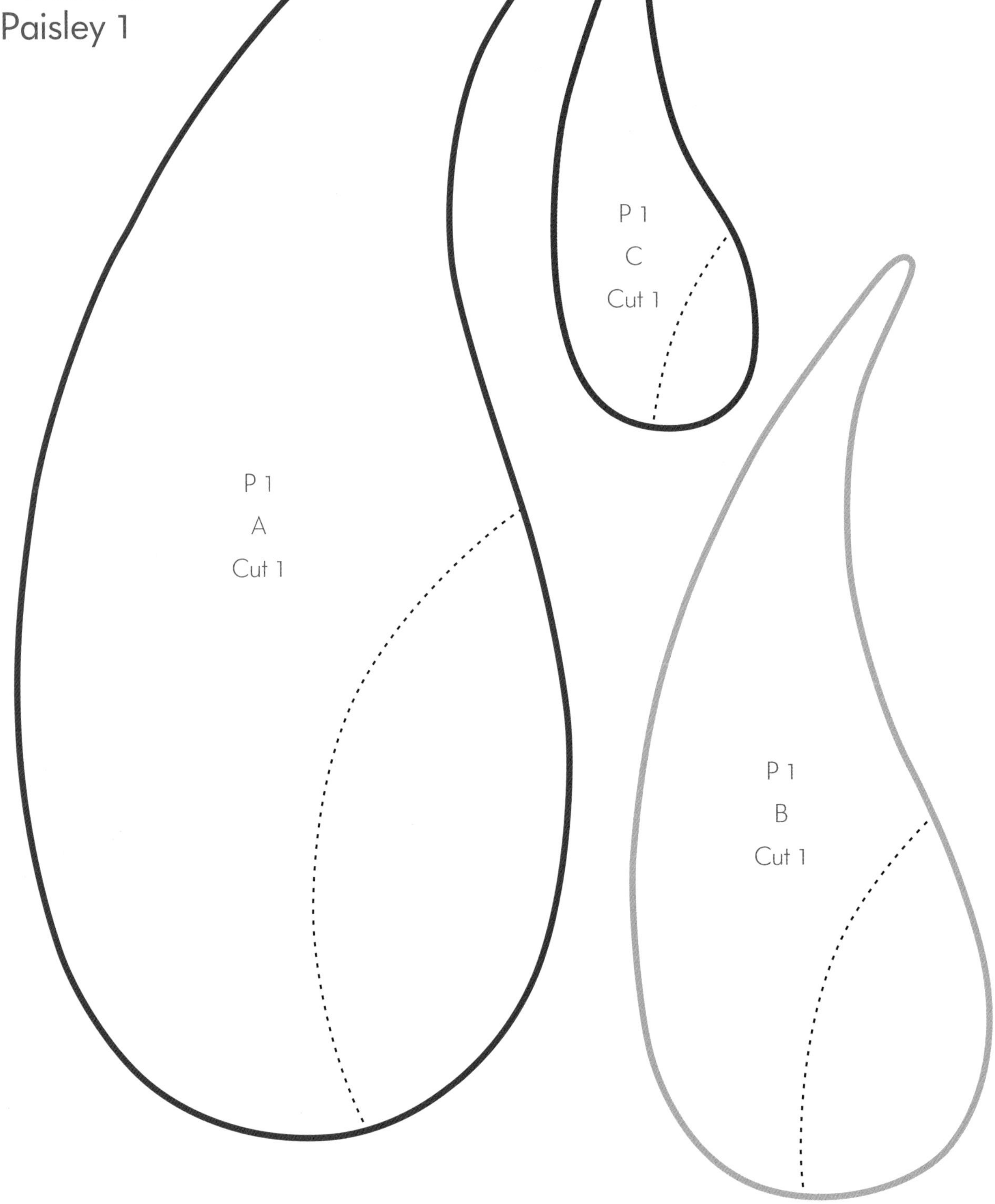

P 1
C
Cut 1

P 1
A
Cut 1

P 1
B
Cut 1

The appliqué shapes will need to be
reversed if using a fusible product.

──────── Cut Lines
---------- Overlay Lines

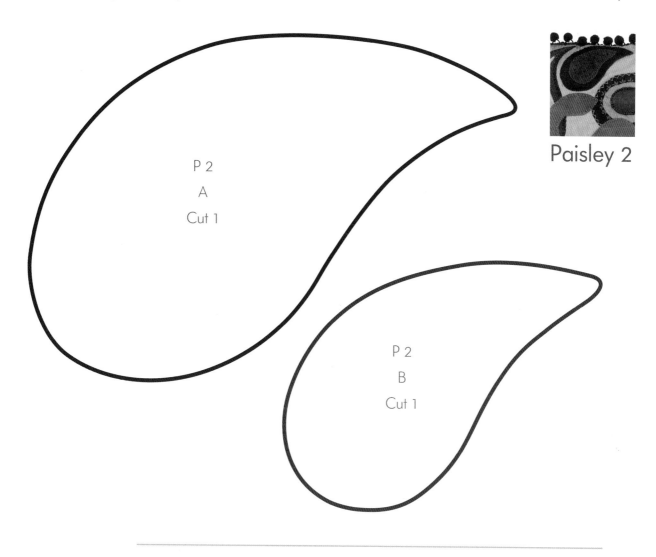

P 2
A
Cut 1

Paisley 2

P 2
B
Cut 1

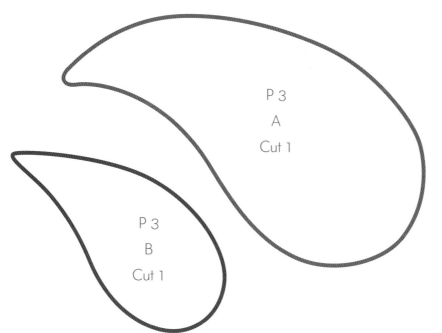

P 3
A
Cut 1

Paisley 3

P 3
B
Cut 1

Cut Lines ━━━━━
Overlay Lines - - - - - - -

The appliqué shapes will need to be
reversed if using a fusible product.

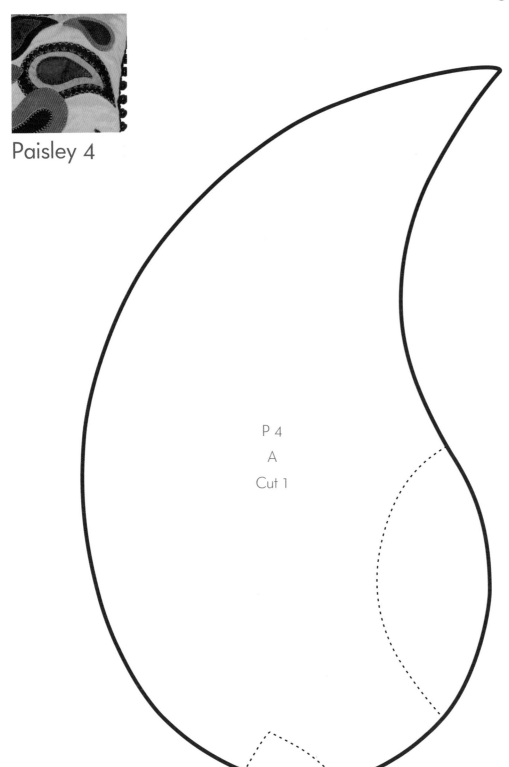

Paisley 4

P 4

A

Cut 1

The appliqué shapes will need to be reversed if using a fusible product.

Cut Lines
Overlay Lines

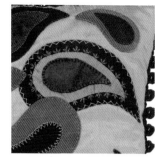

Paisley 4

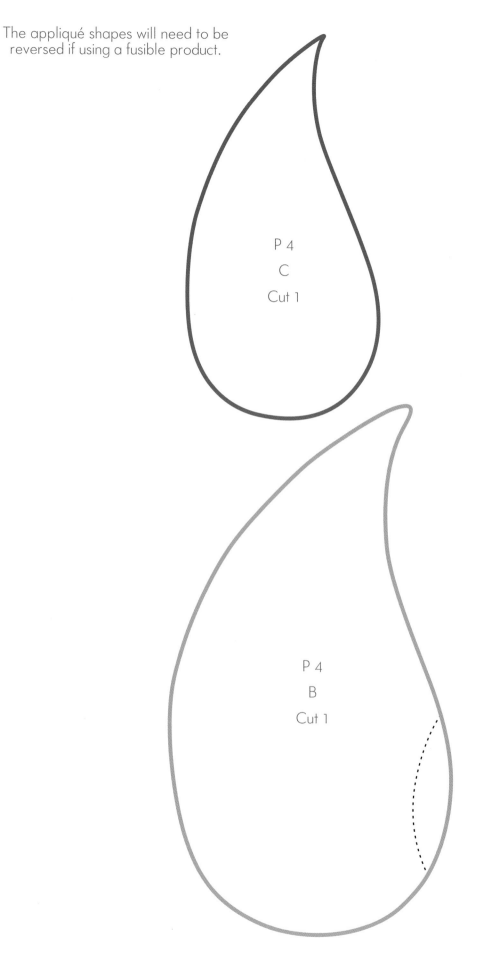

P 4
C
Cut 1

P 4
B
Cut 1

Cut Lines ▬▬▬▬
Overlay Lines ----------

The appliqué shapes will need to be
reversed if using a fusible product.

Paisley 5

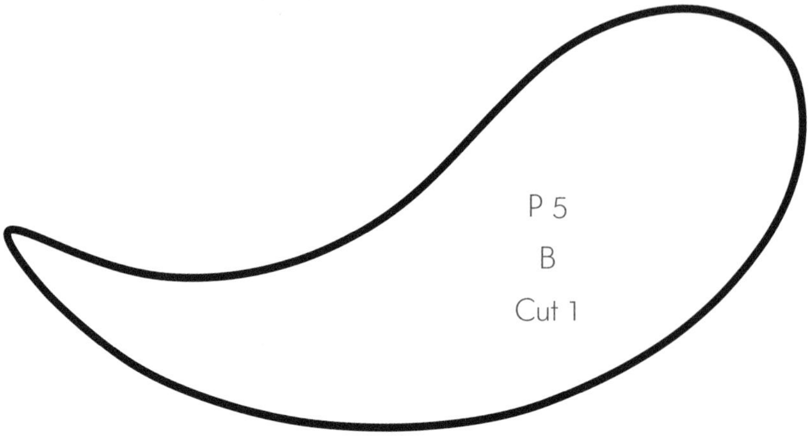

P 5

B

Cut 1

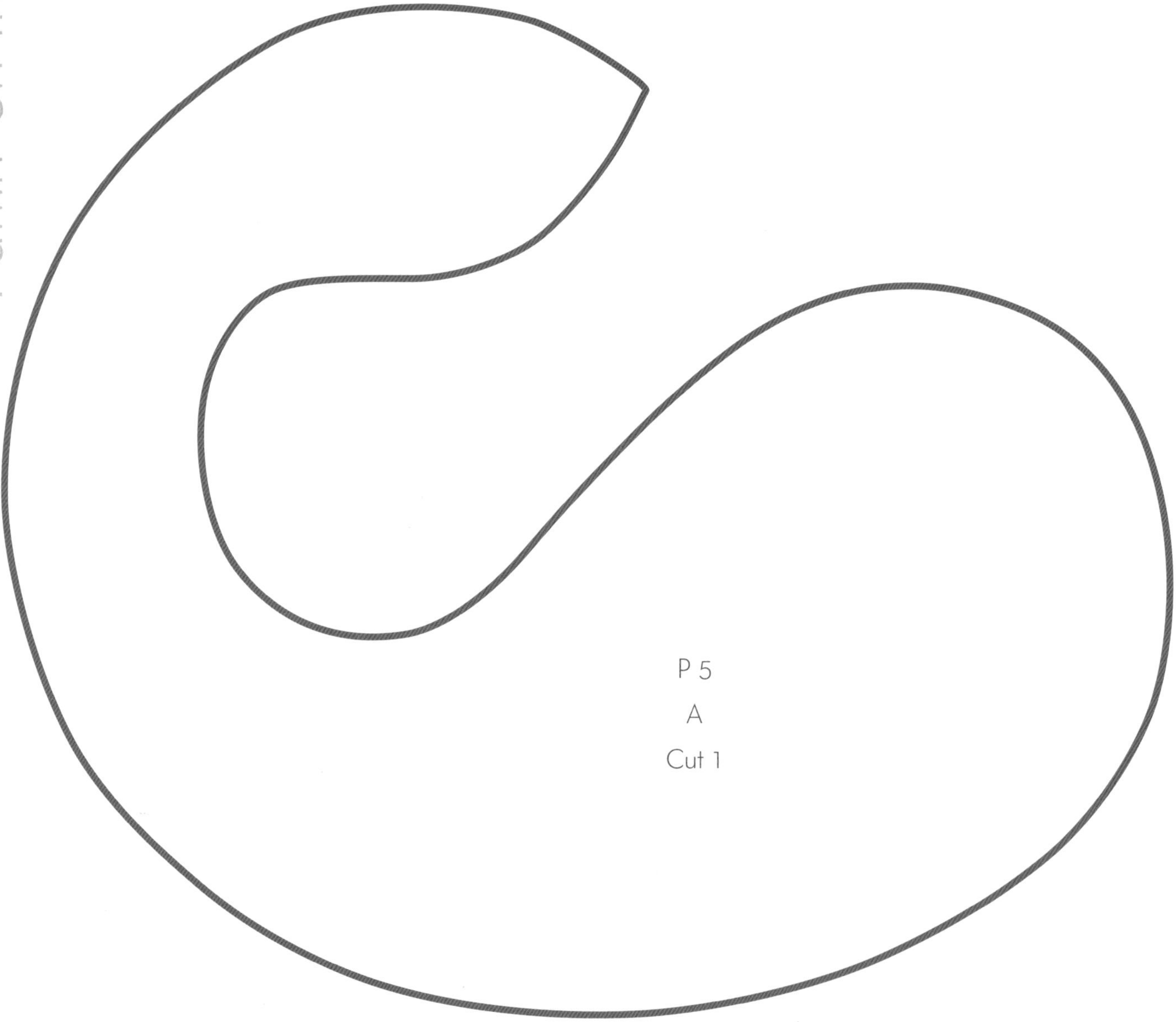

P 5

A

Cut 1

The appliqué shapes will need to be reversed if using a fusible product.

Cut Lines ——————
Overlay Lines ------------

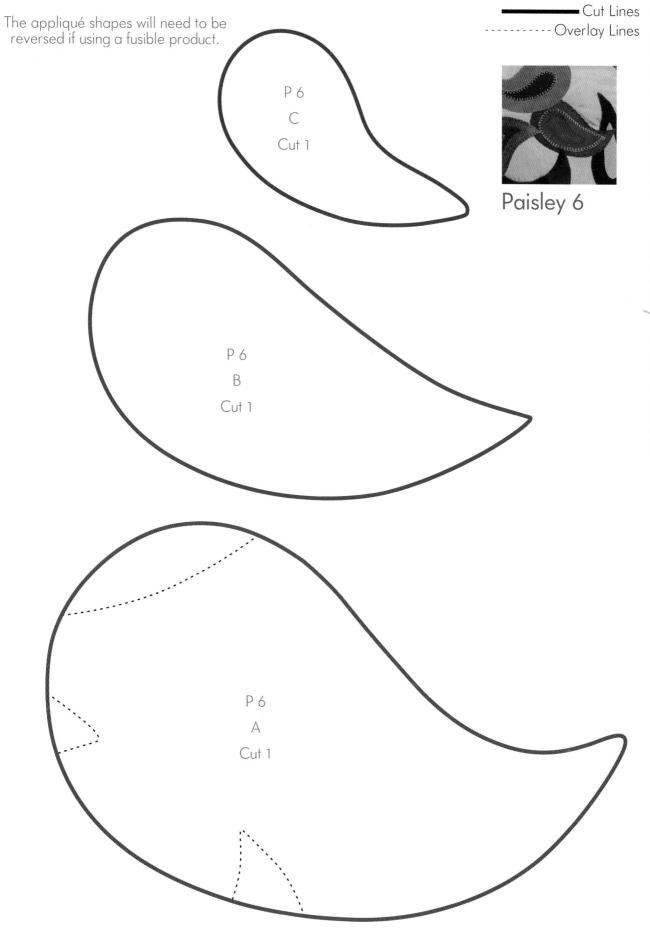

P 6
C
Cut 1

Paisley 6

P 6
B
Cut 1

P 6
A
Cut 1

91

Cut Lines ▬▬▬
Overlay Lines ----------

The appliqué shapes will need to be reversed if using a fusible product.

Paisley 7

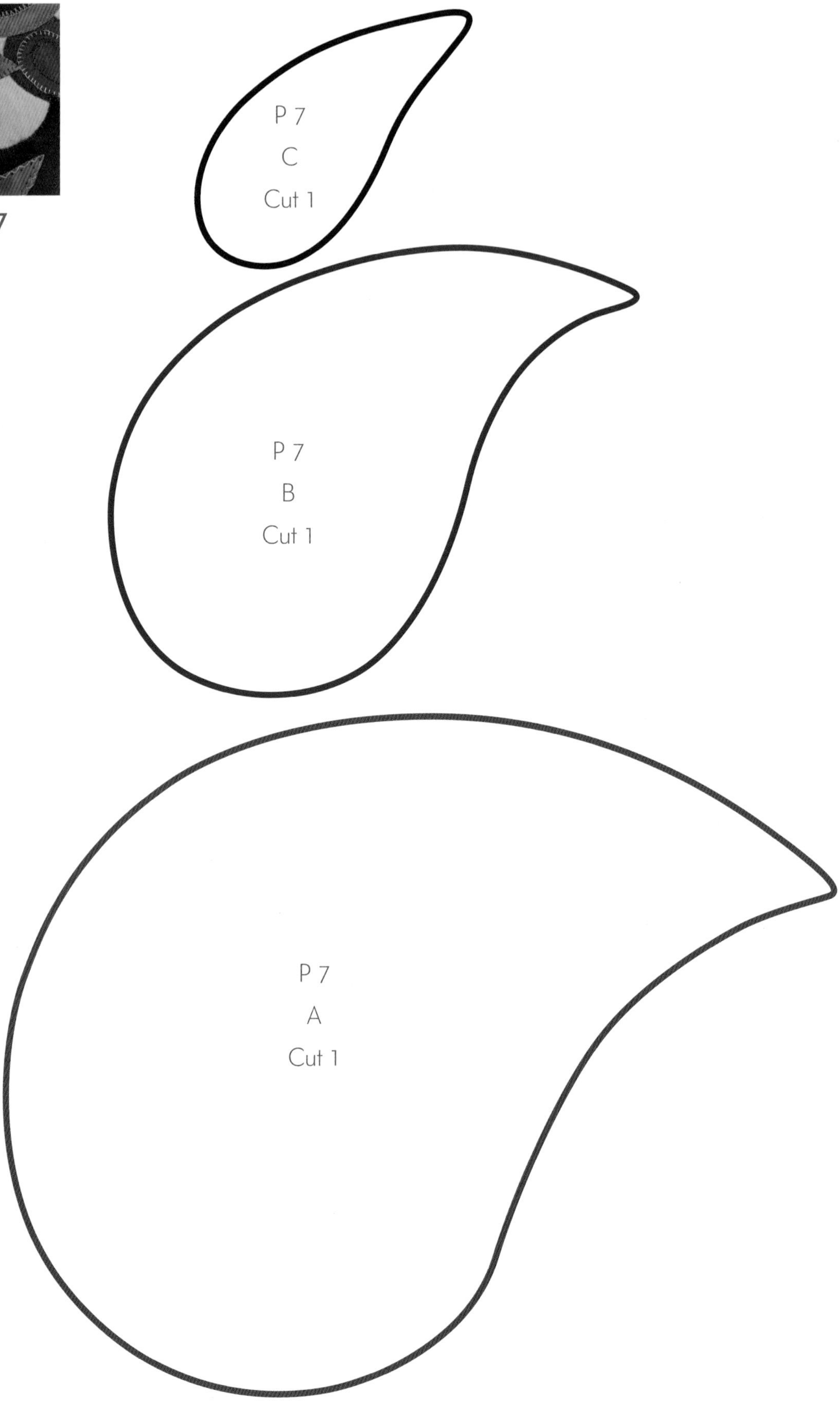

P 7
C
Cut 1

P 7
B
Cut 1

P 7
A
Cut 1

The appliqué shapes will need to be
reversed if using a fusible product. ━━━━━ Cut Lines
········· Overlay Lines

P 8
B
Cut 1

P 8
A
Cut 1

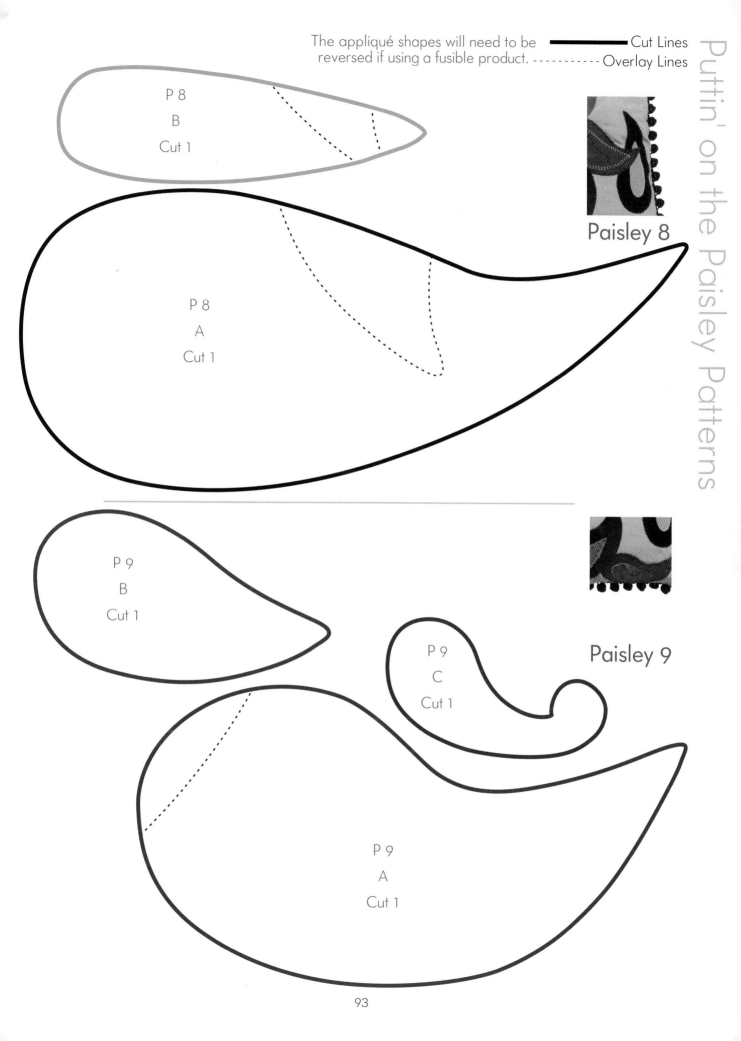

Paisley 8

P 9
B
Cut 1

P 9
C
Cut 1

Paisley 9

P 9
A
Cut 1

Cut Lines ▬▬▬▬
Overlay Lines ----------

The appliqué shapes will need to be
reversed if using a fusible product.

Paisley 10

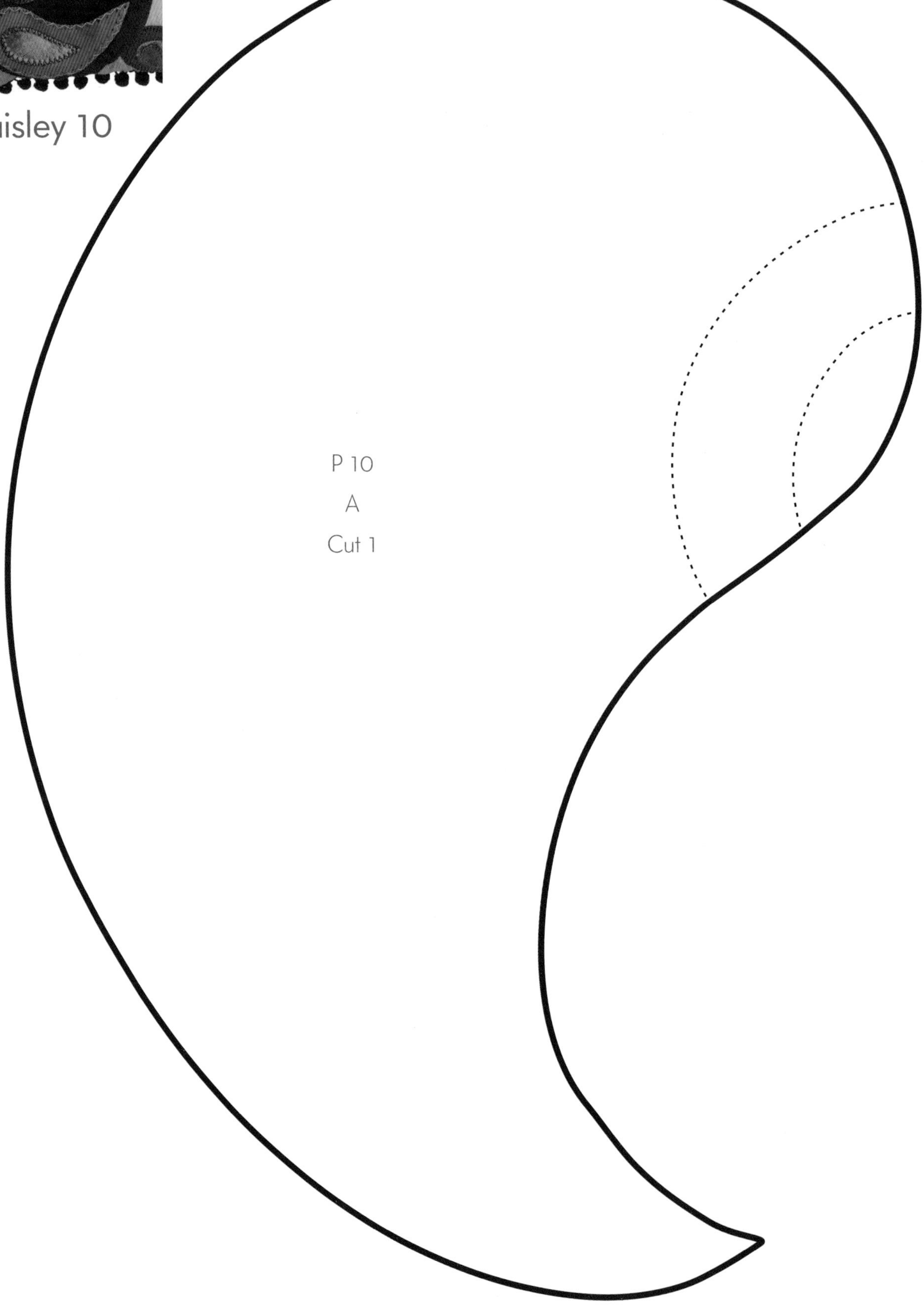

P 10
A
Cut 1

The appliqué shapes will need to be reversed if using a fusible product.

———— Cut Lines
------------ Overlay Lines

Paisley 10

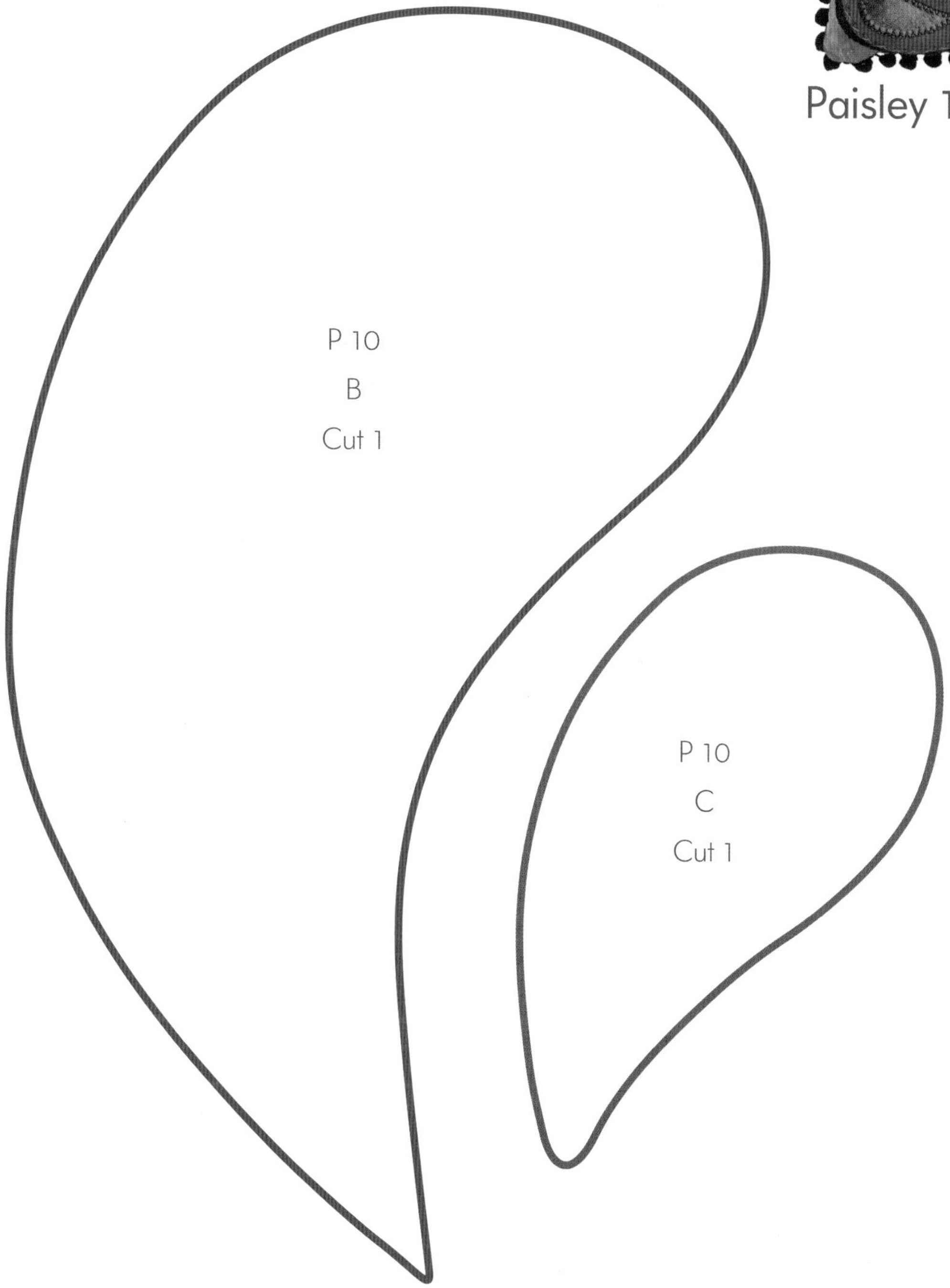

P 10
B
Cut 1

P 10
C
Cut 1

Wool Medallion

A Lap Size Quilt

Finished Size: 48-1/2" x 60-1/2"

A unique collection of wool medallions is featured in this quilt. The colorful spiral appliquéd designs are framed with simple rectangular pieced borders. The Wool Medallion quilt can be used as a wall hanging or lap quilt. Select one medallion design for a pillow front or three to create a table runner.

Materials

Note: Choose your own colors
or refer to the photo for ideas.

Cotton

Background Blocks and Border Rectangles:
(12) 3/8 yard pieces of 12 colors

Inner Border: 1/4 yard

Binding: 1/2 yard

Backing (crosswise seam): 3-1/2 yards
Note: If using a lengthwise seam you will need 4 yards

Wool Appliqué

Block 1

Star: 10" purple square

Bursts: 9" rust square

Drops: 6" teal square

Center Circles: 3" blue square and 3" salmon square

Block 2

Medallion: 12" x 16" rust rectangle

Circle and Diamonds: 8" green square

Center Circle: 2" pink square

Block 3

Medallion: 12" x 16" turquoise rectangle

Circles: 6" orange square

Block 4

Large Medallion: 12" x 16" purple rectangle

Diamond: 3" green square

Small Diamond: 2" yellow square

Block 5

Medallion: 12" x 16" raspberry rectangle

Block 6

Medallion: 12" x 16" coral rectangle

Diamonds: 8" turquoise square

Petals: 8" purple square

Circle: 3" yellow square

Block 7

Medallion: 12" x 16" rust rectangle

Small Center Circle: 3" blue square

Large Center Circle: 3" light coral square

Outer Circles: 6" orange square

Block 8

Medallion: 12" x 16" light coral rectangle

Ovals: 6" turquoise square

Center Circle: 3" orange square

Block 9

Medallion: 12" x 16" teal rectangle

Center Circle: 3" green square

Circles: 6" magenta square

Block 10

Rim: 12" x 16" blue rectangle

Hearts: 8" light coral square

Star: 6" purple square

Large Circle Center: 3" teal square

Small Circle Center: 3" orange square

Mini Circles: 6" lime square

Block 11

Medallion: 12" x 16" aqua rectangle

Large Center Circle: 4" raspberry square

Small Center Circle: 2" yellow square

Block 12

Medallion: 12" x 16" green rectangle

Ovals: 6" gold square

Large Center Circle: 4" rust square

Small Center Circle: 3" purple square

Appliqué Patterns
Pages 100-111

Additional Materials
Batting: 60" x 72" rectangle

Floss, perle cotton or wool threads

Chenille needle size 24

Basic sewing supplies

Refer to pages 6-12 before beginning the project.

wof = width of fabric

Cutting Instructions

From **each** 12 block/border fabric, cut:
(1) 12-1/2" block square
(1) 5-1/2" x 8-1/2" border rectangle
(1) 5-1/2" x 10-1/2" border rectangle
Note: 2 will be extra.

From inner border fabric, cut:
(5) 1-1/2" x wof strips.
Sew the strips together end-to-end and cut:
(2) 1-1/2" x 48-1/2" side inner border strips
(2) 1-1/2" x 38-1/2" top/bottom inner
border strips

From binding fabric, cut:
(6) 2-1/2" x wof strips

From backing fabric, cut:
(2) 42" x 63" rectangles (crosswise seam)
OR (2) 30" x 72" rectangles (lengthwise seam)

Preparing the Appliqué

1. Using the shapes on pages 100-111 and referring to pages 8-10, prepare the appliqué shapes.

2. Referring to the photo on page 96 and the Quilt Assembly Diagram on page 99, place the shapes on the 12-1/2" block squares. Refer to Layered Shapes on page 11.

3. Stitch the shapes to the block squares. Refer to pages 11-12 for stitching ideas.

Piecing the Outer Borders

1. Sew (5) 5-1/2" x 10-1/2" border rectangles together along the short edges to make a side outer border strip. Make 2 side outer border strips. The strips should measure 5-1/2" x 50-1/2".

2. Sew (6) 5-1/2" x 8-1/2" border rectangles together along the short edges to make a top/bottom outer border strip. Make 2 top/bottom outer border strips. The strips should measure 5-1/2" x 48-1/2".

Assembly Instructions

1. Referring to the Quilt Assembly Diagram on page 99, lay out the 12 medallion blocks in 4 rows with 3 blocks in each row.

2. Sew the blocks together in rows. Sew the rows together to complete the quilt center.

3. Sew the 1-1/2" x 48-1/2" side inner border strips to opposite sides of the quilt center.

4. Sew the 1-1/2" x 38-1/2" top/bottom inner border strips to the top and bottom of the quilt center.

5. Sew the 5-1/2" x 50-1/2" side outer border strips to the opposite sides of the quilt center.

6. Sew the 5-1/2" x 48-1/2" top/bottom outer border strips to the top and bottom of the quilt center to complete the quilt top.

Finishing the Quilt

1. Layer the quilt top, batting and backing.

2. Hand-baste or pin the three layers together. Hand- or machine-quilt.

3. Sew the (6) 2-1/2" x wof binding strips together to make one continuous strip.

4. Trim the extra batting and backing even with the edges of the quilt top.

5. Sew the binding to the edges of the quilt top.

6. Turn the binding over the edge to the back and hand- or machine-stitch in place.

Quilt Assembly Diagram

Cut Lines ▬▬▬▬
Overlay Lines ----------

Block 1

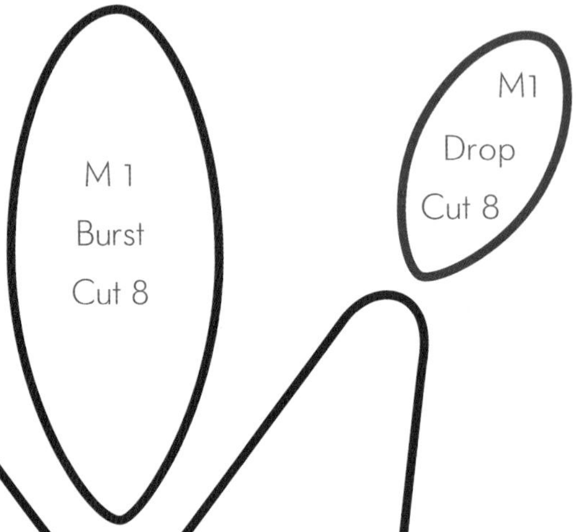

M 1
Burst
Cut 8

M1
Drop
Cut 8

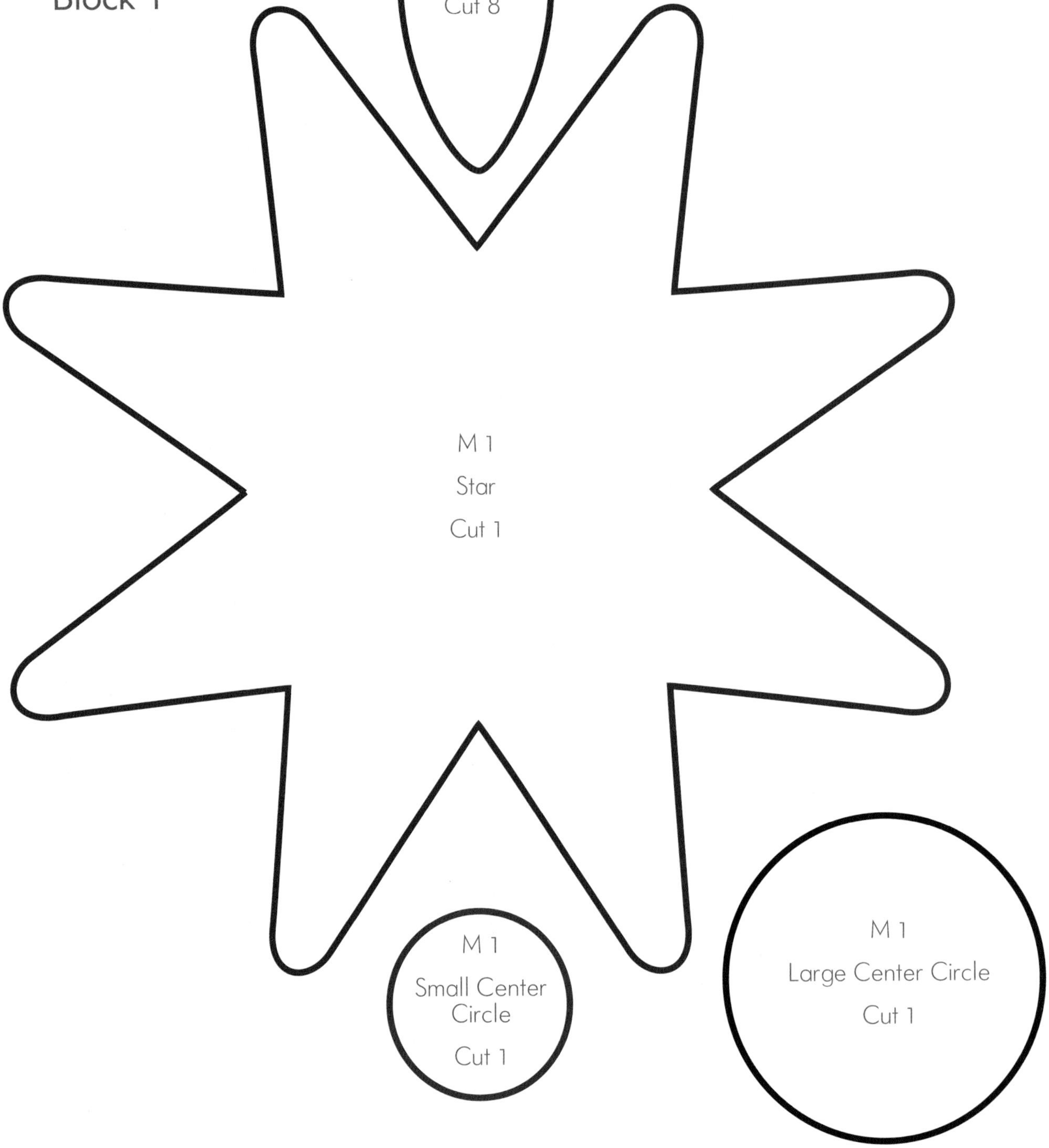

M 1
Star
Cut 1

M 1
Small Center
Circle
Cut 1

M 1
Large Center Circle
Cut 1

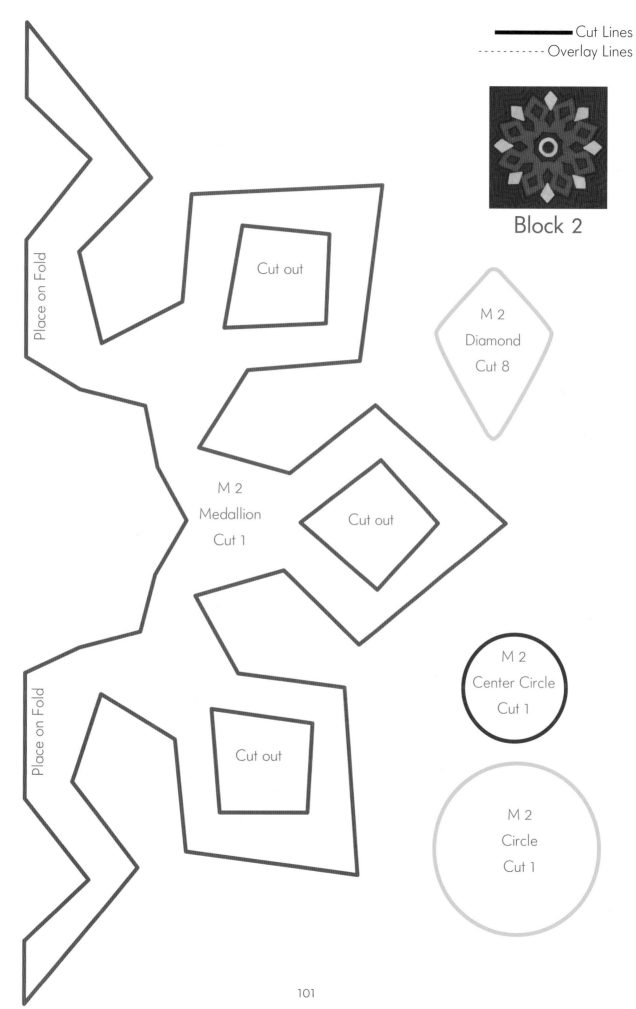

Cut Lines
Overlay Lines

Block 2

Place on Fold

Cut out

M 2
Diamond
Cut 8

M 2
Medallion
Cut 1

Cut out

M 2
Center Circle
Cut 1

Place on Fold

Cut out

M 2
Circle
Cut 1

Wool Medallion Patterns

Cut Lines ━━━━
Overlay Lines - - - - - - - - - -

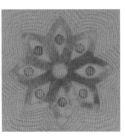

Block 3

M 3
Circle
Cut 8

Cut out

Place on Fold

M 3
Medallion
Cut 1

Cut out

Cut out

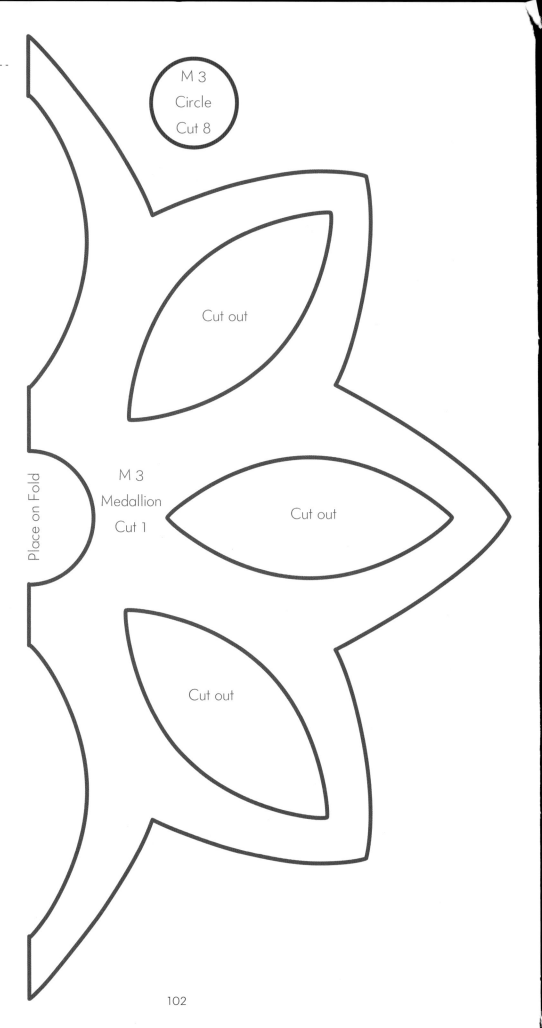

Cut Lines
---------- Overlay Lines

Block 4

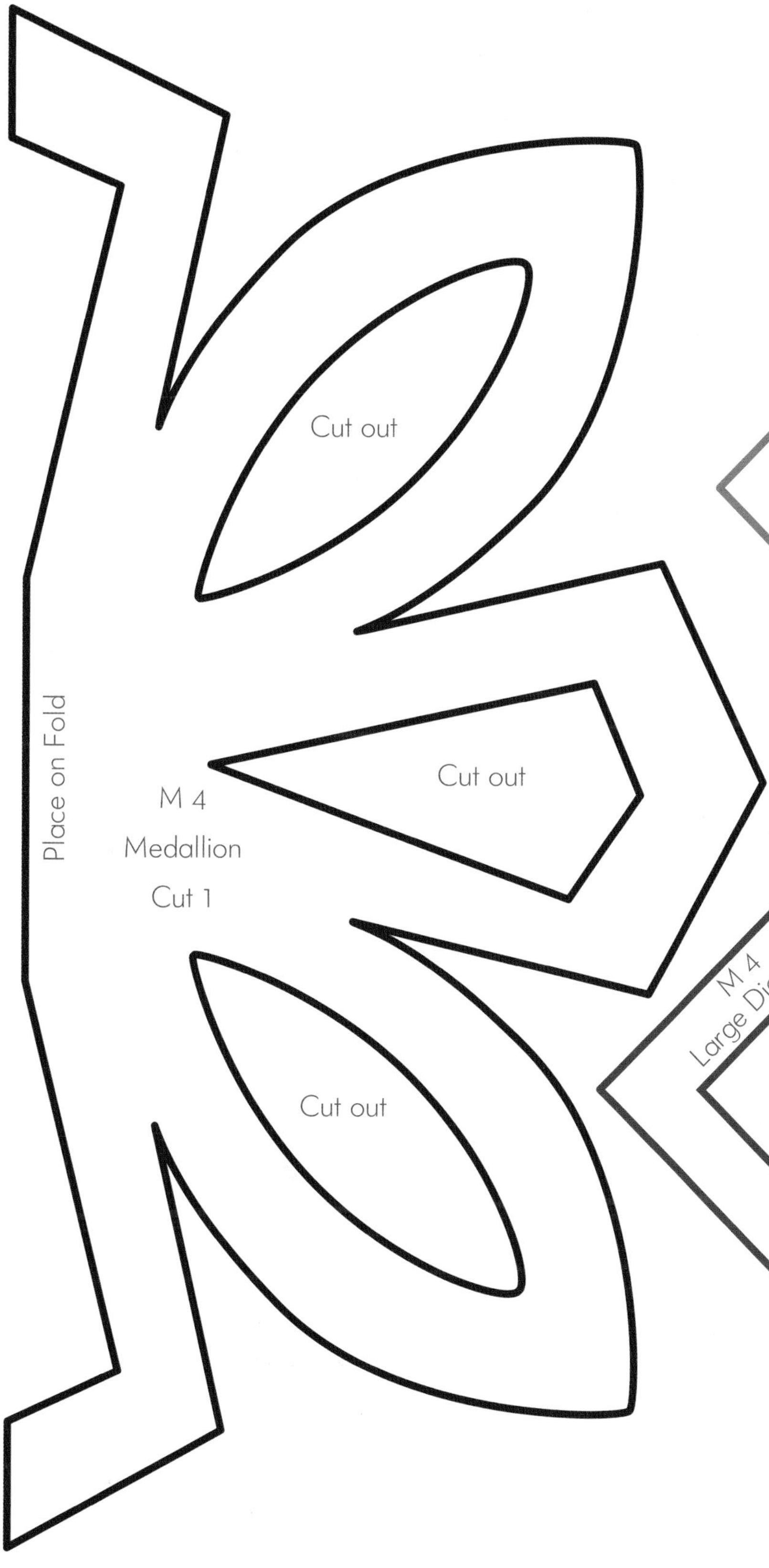

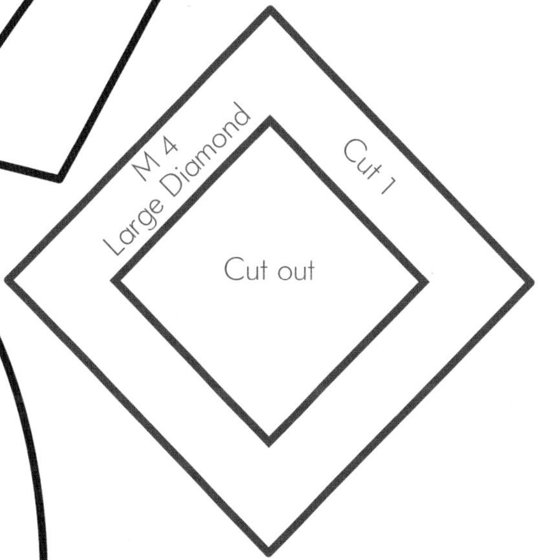

Cut out

M 4
Small
Diamond
Cut 1

M 4
Medallion
Cut 1

Place on Fold

Cut out

Cut out

M 4
Large Diamond

Cut 1

Cut out

Cut Lines ▬▬▬
Overlay Lines ----------

Block 5

M 5
Medallion
Cut 1

Place on Fold

Cut out

Cut out

Cut out

Cut out

Cut out

Cut out

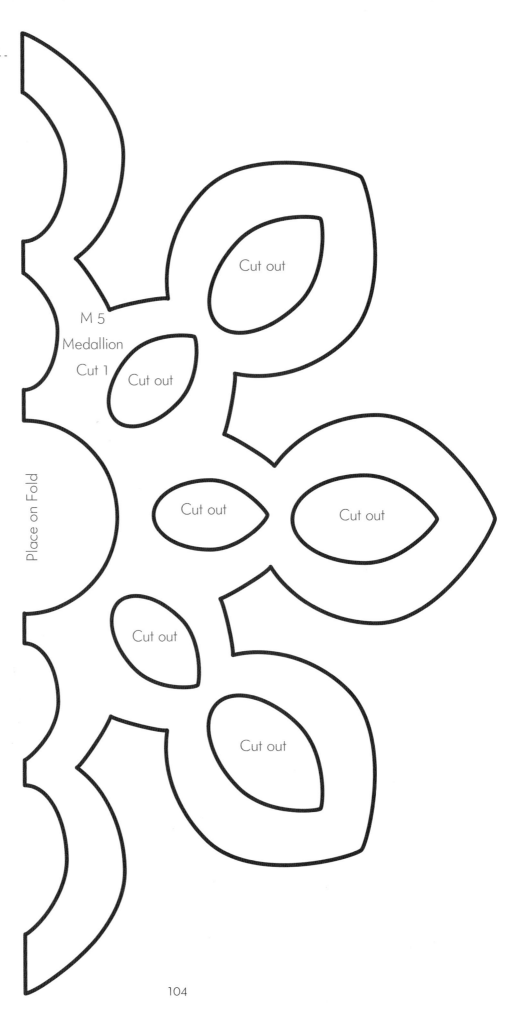

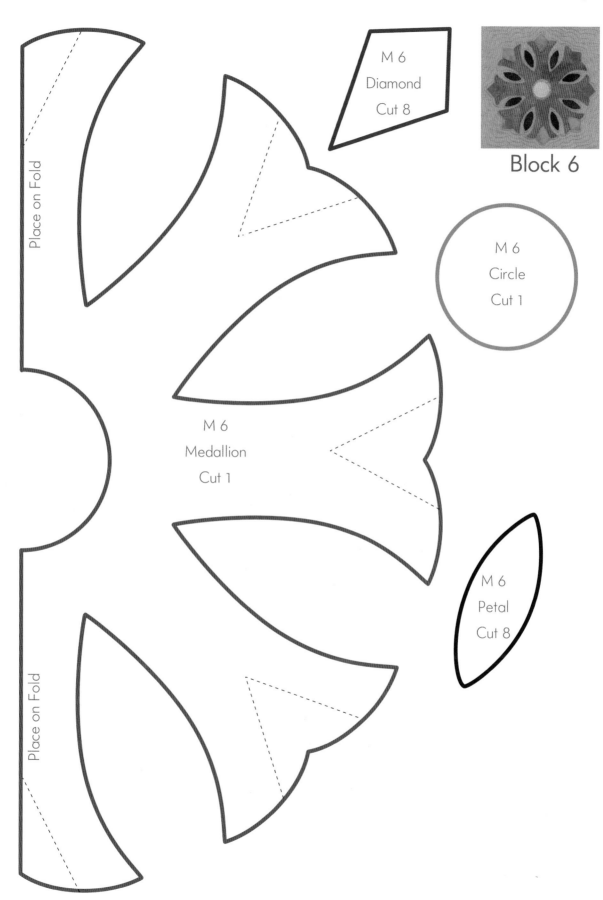

Cut Lines
Overlay Lines

M 6
Diamond
Cut 8

Block 6

M 6
Circle
Cut 1

M 6
Medallion
Cut 1

M 6
Petal
Cut 8

Place on Fold

Place on Fold

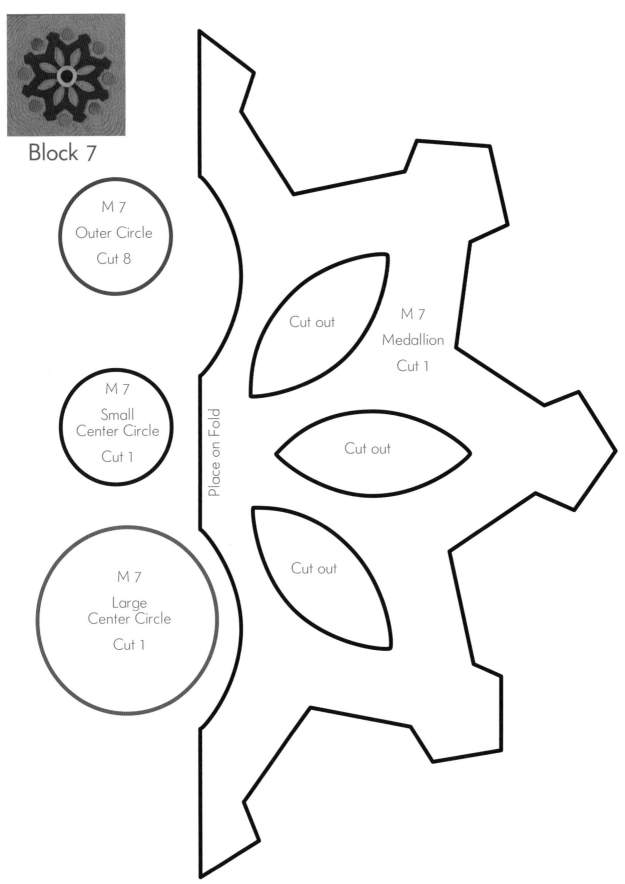

Cut Lines ━━━━━━
Overlay Lines ----------

Block 7

M 7
Outer Circle
Cut 8

M 7
Small
Center Circle
Cut 1

M 7
Large
Center Circle
Cut 1

Place on Fold

Cut out

M 7
Medallion
Cut 1

Cut out

Cut out

Cut Lines
Overlay Lines

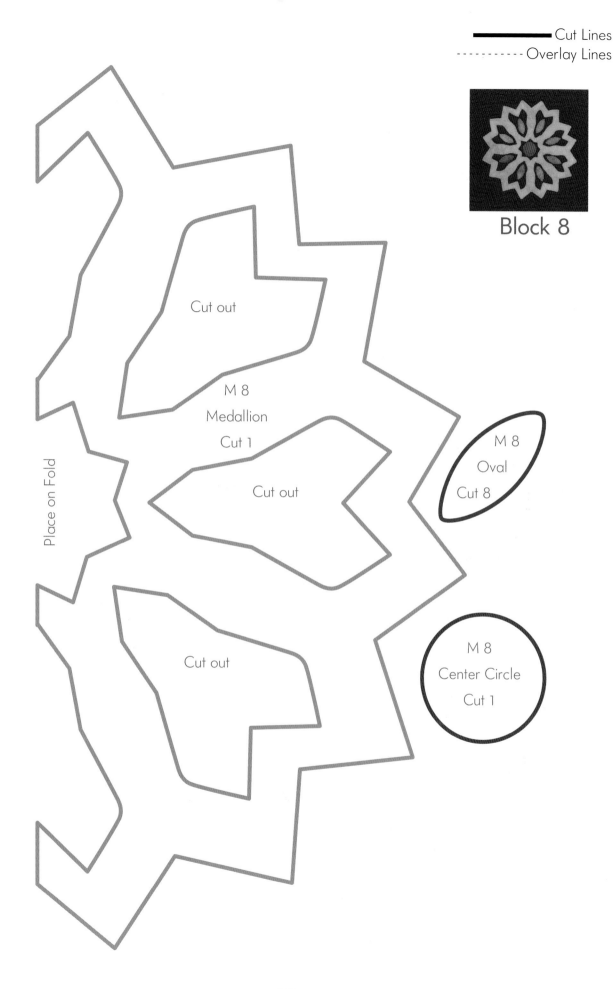

Block 8

Cut out

M 8

Medallion

Cut 1

Cut out

M 8
Oval
Cut 8

Place on Fold

Cut out

M 8
Center Circle
Cut 1

Cut Lines ━━━━━
Overlay Lines ----------

Block 9

Wool Medallion Patterns

M 9
Center Circle
Cut 1

Place on Fold

M 9
Circle
Cut 8

Cut
out

Cut
out

Cut
out

M 9
Medallion
Cut 1

Cut
out

Cut
out

Cut
out

Cut
out

Cut Lines
Overlay Lines

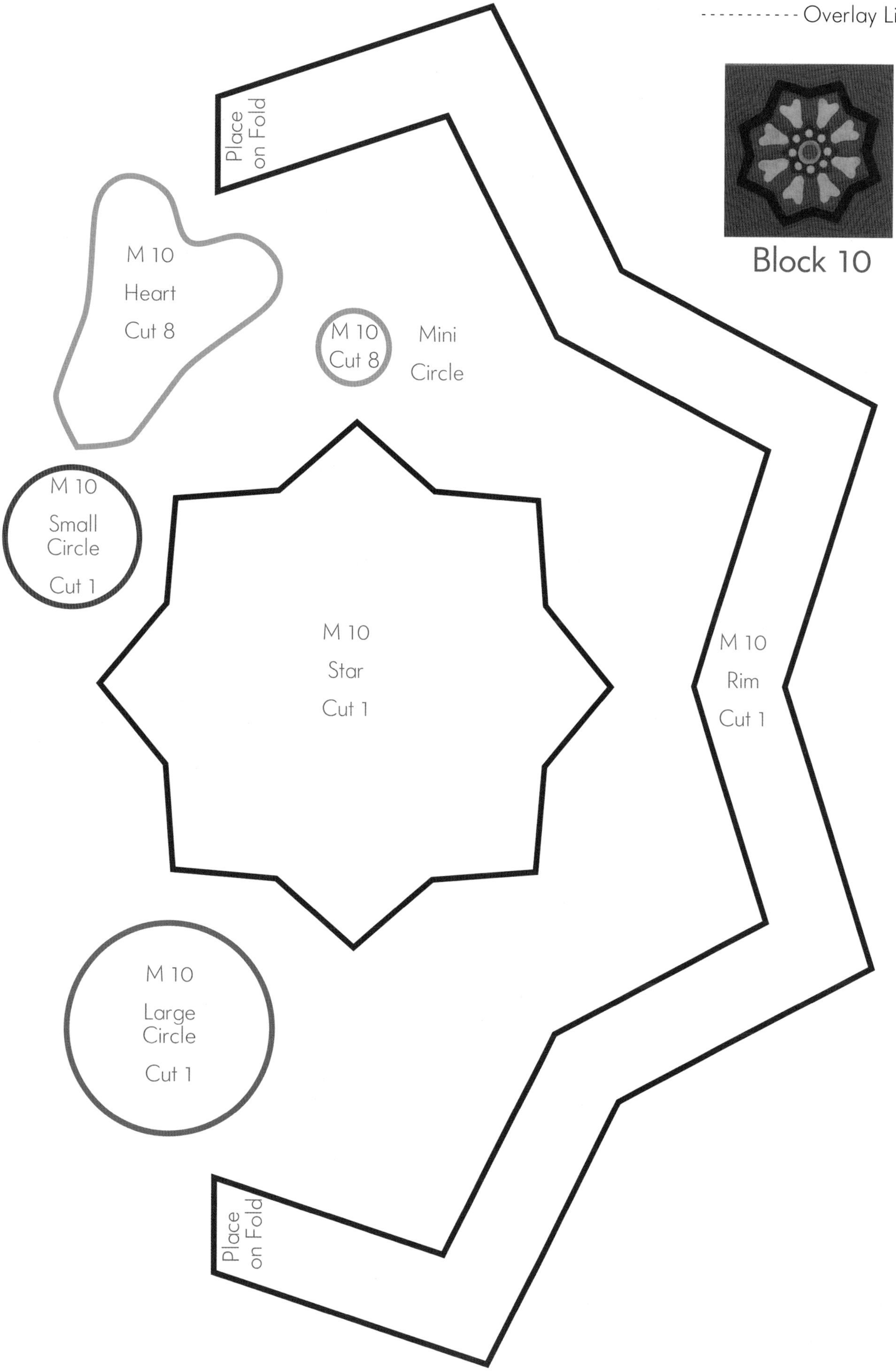

Block 10

M 10
Heart
Cut 8

M 10
Cut 8

Mini
Circle

M 10
Small
Circle
Cut 1

M 10
Star
Cut 1

M 10
Rim
Cut 1

M 10
Large
Circle
Cut 1

Place on Fold

Place
on Fold

Wool Medallion Patterns

Cut Lines ▬▬
Overlay Lines ----------

Block 11

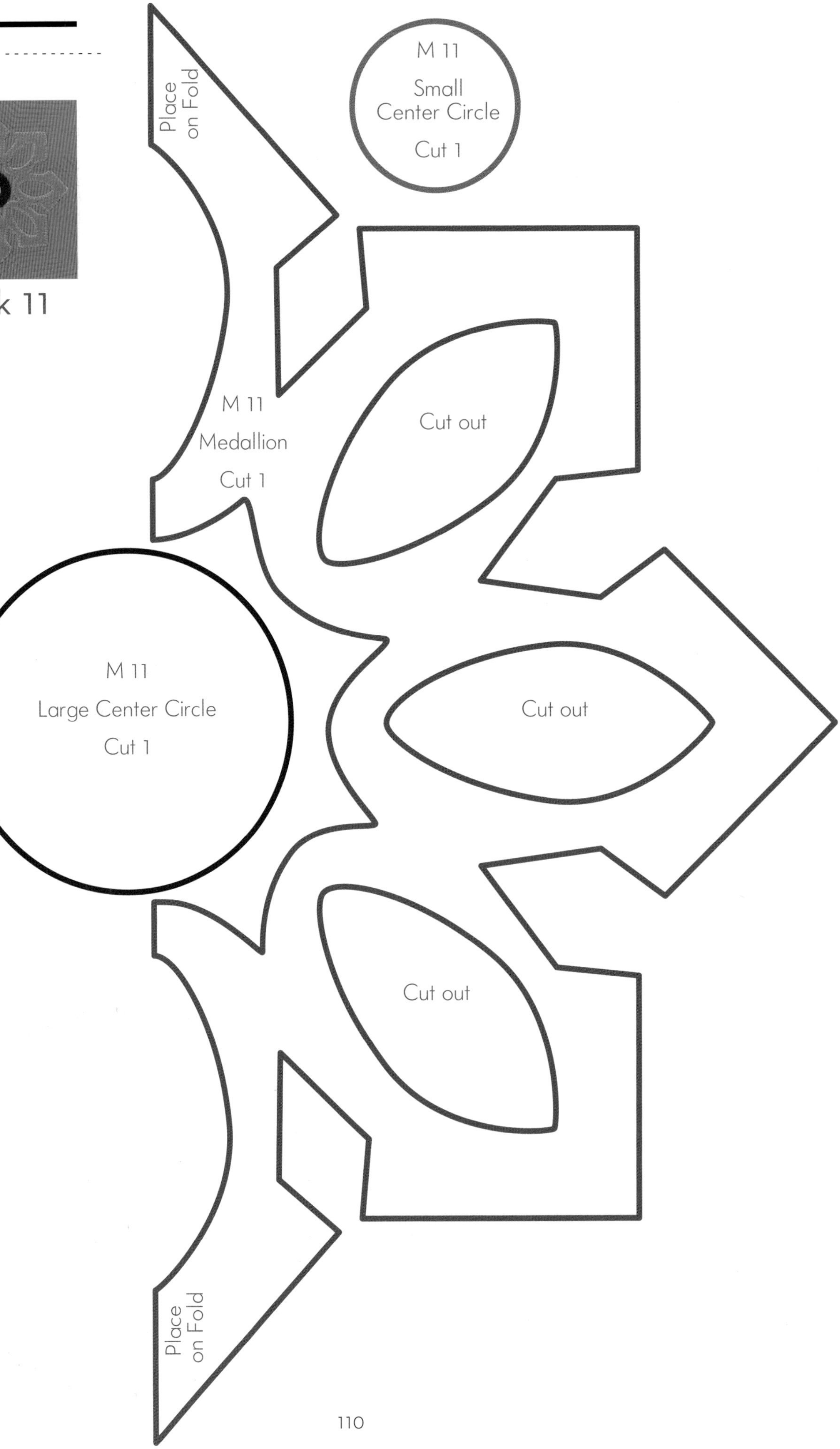

Place on Fold

M 11
Small
Center Circle
Cut 1

M 11
Medallion
Cut 1

Cut out

Cut out

M 11
Large Center Circle
Cut 1

Cut out

Place
on Fold

110

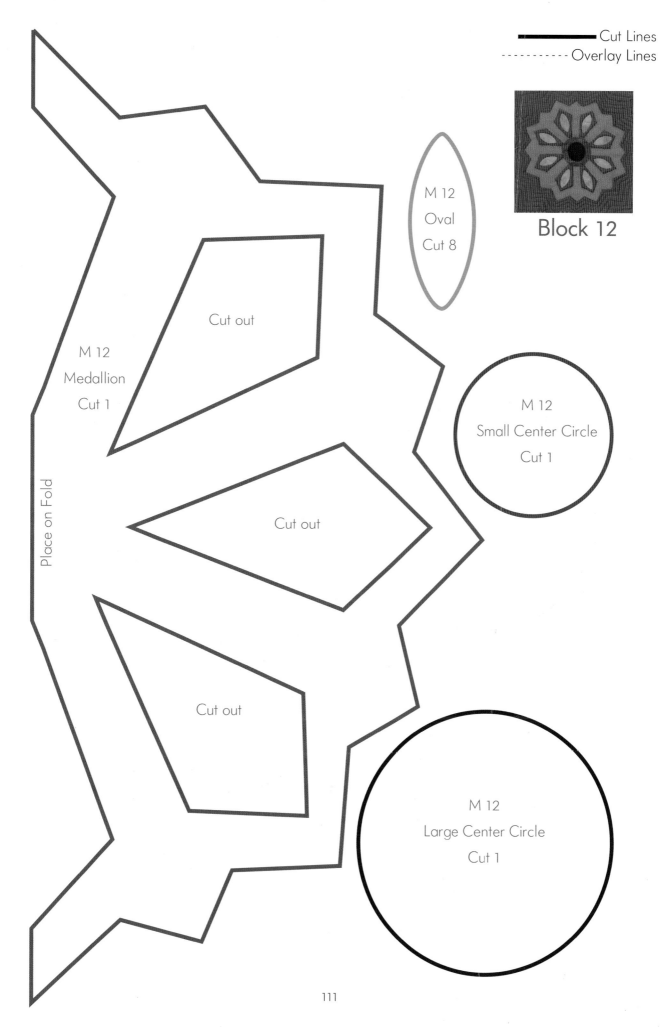

Cut Lines
Overlay Lines

Block 12

M 12
Oval
Cut 8

M 12
Small Center Circle
Cut 1

M 12
Medallion
Cut 1

Cut out

Cut out

Cut out

Place on Fold

M 12
Large Center Circle
Cut 1

About the Author

Angela is a designer, author and instructor and has been quilting for more than 25 years. In 2005, she established her pattern company, Appliqué After Hours. After many years of teaching needleturn appliqué, Angela authored her first book, *Needleturn Appliqué, The Basics & Beyond*, in 2012. Recently, she has ventured into the world of wool appliqué, providing her with yet another avenue of artistic expression.

Residents of Des Moines, Iowa, Angela and her husband, Bill, are currently enjoying their recent change of status to "empty nesters" after raising six children. They are also the proud grandparents of four grandchildren.

Acknowledgments

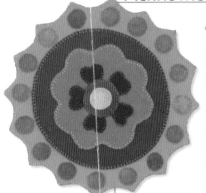

A special "Thank You" to the following:

My loving husband, Bill, who gives me endless guidance and encouragement.

My good friend, Patty Barrett, for her support and professional advice.

Landauer Publishing for their dedication, expertise and talent

Resources

Threads
Sulky—100% Mercerized Cotton, 12 wt.
www.sulky.com

DMC Perle Cotton Thread
www.dmc-usa.com

Finca Threads by Presencia,
Perle Cotton
www.colonialneedle.com/
Presencia-America

Aurifil Mako Thread
www.aurifil.com

Valdani Perle Cotton Threads
www.valdani.com

Genziana Wool Thread
www.tristan.bc.ca

Embroidery Floss
DMC Embroidery Floss
www.dmc-usa.com

Scissors
Famoré Cutlery 6"
Large Ring Comfort Handle
www.famorecutlery.com

Needles & Appliqué Pins
Jeana Kimball Fox Cottage Needles
www.jeanakimballquilter.com

Clover Needles and Appliqué Pins
www.clover-usa.com

Needle Threader
Needle Threader by LoRan
www.dritz.com/quilting-sewing-
supplies/loran-needlecraft

Fusible Products
Lite Steam- A-Seam 2, Trans Web
www.warmcompany.com

Soft Fuse
www.SoftFusePremium.com

Craf-Tex Interlining
www.bosalonline.com

Landauer Publishing wishes to thank Polk County Master Gardeners, RS Welding Studio, West End Salvage and The Woolen Needle for allowing us to use photographs taken at their sites.

For more wool appliqué patterns and inspiration visit
Angela's website, Appliqué After Hours at www.appliquéafterhours.com